Restorative Assessment

Strength-Based Practices That Support All Learners

Laura M. Greenstein

CORWIN

A SAGE Publishing Company

FOR INFORMATION:

Corwin

A SAGE Company

2455 Teller Road

Thousand Oaks, California 91320

(800) 233-9936

www.corwin.com

SAGE Publications Ltd.

1 Oliver's Yard

55 City Road

London EC1Y 1SP

United Kingdom

SAGE Publications India Pvt. Ltd.

B 1/I 1 Mohan Cooperative Industrial Area

Mathura Road, New Delhi 110 044

India

SAGE Publications Asia-Pacific Pte. Ltd.

3 Church Street

#10-04 Samsung Hub

Singapore 049483

Program Director: Jessica Allan

Associate Editor: Lucas Schleicher

Senior Editorial Assistant: Katie Crilley

Production Editor: Amy Schroller

Copy Editor: Diane Wainwright

Typesetter: C&M Digitals (P) Ltd.

Proofreader: Dennis W. Webb

Indexer: Rick Hurd

Cover Designer: Michael Dubowe

Marketing Manager: Nicole Franks

Printed in the United States of America

Library of Congress Cataloging-in-Publication Data

Names: Greenstein, Laura, author.

Title: Restorative assessment : strength-based practices that support all learners / Laura M. Greenstein.

Description: Thousand Oaks, California : Corwin, 2018. | Includes bibliographical references and index.

Identifiers: LCCN 2017017294 | ISBN 9781506390253 (pbk. : alk. paper)

Subjects: LCSH: Educational tests and measurements—Methodology. | Educational evaluation—Methodology. | Students—Rating of—Methodology.

Classification: LCC LB3051 .G717 2017 | DDC 371.26—dc23 LC record available at https://lccn.loc.gov/2017017294

This book is printed on acid-free paper.

Certified Chain of Custody
Promoting Sustainable Forestry
www.sfiprogram.org
SFI-01268

SFI label applies to text stock

17 18 19 20 21 10 9 8 7 6 5 4 3 2 1

Contents

Preface

I grew up in a big city, the child of immigrants who barely achieved an eighth-grade education. I was fortunate in that they believed in the value of learning and provided the encouragement and support it took for me to succeed. This is not the case for many children growing up in poverty, who come from another country and culture, who move frequently, experience profound stress, or live with families for whom daily life is a struggle.

Please understand that I am not passing judgment but rather relying on the data that say for millions of children, getting to school, paying attention, and monitoring behavior is a daily challenge. For these children, learning is not at the top of their priorities and testing is of little concern. I have listened to arguments that we should not identify subgroups, as it leads to labeling and ultimately discrimination. Nor do I believe that striving for equality where every student receives the same input (that is, curriculum, resources, and instruction) and is taught in the same way is the answer. Rather, this book is about equity: Providing the resources and supports that each child needs to succeed. It is about honoring the uniqueness of each child, giving credence to their needs, and responding in ways that educationally uplift them.

Success looks different for every learner. For Monty, it means getting himself to school; for Natasha, it means finding joy in learning something new; and for Xavier, it requires a commitment to the hard work it takes to see incremental daily progress. These changes didn't come easily for any of them, nor for the many other students who feel disconnected, disenfranchised, and overwhelmed.

I am indebted to my advisory board for recommending this topic. Through their experiences working with at-risk students, the disengaged, and families living in poverty, they reminded me that, while failure is not an option, success is hard work that comes in small steps. I am grateful for their insights on why noncognitive attributes and dispositions are just as important as intellectual skills in helping every learner reach his or her potential. This book seeks to find that fine balance so that all students can be successful.

Pixabay

Acknowledgments

This book would not be possible without the many teachers who took a leap into these divergent strategies and the untold number of students who realized success with these restorative approaches to assessment.

I am also grateful for

- the enduring support of family: Eric, my spouse of many decades, my children Andrew and Casey, and extended family everywhere who continue to inspire and support me;

- the encouragement and insights of my advisory board;

- and of course, the reviewers, project managers, and editors at Corwin.

You have no idea the power you have; it delights my heart to encourage you to continue.

—Maya Angelou

Pixabay

Publisher's Acknowledgments

Corwin gratefully acknowledges the contributions of the following reviewers:

D. Allan Bruner
Science Chair and Chemistry Teacher
Colton High School
Colton, OR

Sister Camille Anne Campbell
President
Mount Carmel Academy
New Orleans, LA

Tamara Daugherty
Art Teacher
Lakeville Elementary
Apopka, FL

Julie Frederick
Teacher, Nationally Board Certified
Seattle Public Schools
Seattle, WA

Renee Peoples
Teaching and Learning Coach
Swain West Elementary
Bryson City, NC

Diane Smith
Retired School Counselor
Smethport Area School District
Smethport, PA

About the Author

Laura M. Greenstein has been an educator for more than 30 years, serving as a teacher, department chair, and school leader in multiple grades and subjects. She combines this background with her experience as a school board member and professional development specialist to bring fresh and original ideas to educators about teaching, learning, and assessing. She consults with schools and districts, and presents at workshops and conferences locally and nationally.

As an adjunct professor at the University of Connecticut and the University of New Haven, she teaches human development and assessment to undergraduate and graduate students, and more recently, teaching, learning, and assessing with technology in the sixth-year digital literacy program. She has a BS from the University of Connecticut, an MS from the State University of New York at Oneonta in education, a sixth year from Sacred Heart University in administration, and an EdD from Johnson and Wales University in educational leadership.

Her website (http://www.assessmentnetwork.net) is a valuable source of information on issues and topics in assessment. She is the author of *What Teachers Really Need to Know About Formative Assessment* from ASCD, *Assessing 21st Century Skills* with Corwin, and *Sticky Assessment: Classroom Strategies to Amplify Student Learning* with Routledge. You can follow her on Twitter @lauragteacher and e-mail her at laura.m.greenstein@gmail.com.

Introduction

Bring together the best practice in teaching, learning, and assessing

Return assessment to its roots through principled and purposeful practice

Nurture an inclusive and sustainable assessment climate

Tests are neither good nor bad—it is the purpose, effect, and use of the tests

Restorative assessment works for all learners

REAL LEARNING

In education, it is understood that the greatest learning takes place when the purpose is clear, prior knowledge is activated, growth is monitored, students are engaged and supported, functional feedback is provided, and multiple assessment methods are used. No wonder students get frustrated when they are told that today they will learn about the Renaissance, are asked what they know about it, complete structured notes on a video, and at the conclusion take a multiple-choice test.

Even when teachers strive to incorporate the best practices into their lessons, students don't always learn. When Emanuel encounters a collection of materials from nature on the table, his first impulse is to touch them, tap one with another, and toss the feather in the air to see if it flies. But the teacher has different plans for sorting the natural resources into boxes by category: plants, animals, minerals, and so forth. So he sits quietly but distractedly as he looks through the window and watches the class next door going on a nature scavenger hunt. Later, he hears them playing classification bingo and talking about their learning as they sort their findings into categories.

Pixabay

Learning is a natural process. Humans are naturally curious. And curiosity sustains learning (von Stumm, Hell, & Chamorro-Premuzic, 2011). For many students, schools stifle that curiosity by being answer-centered. In my experience, schools that are lower performing make teaching and learning even less flexible. In some cases, they have predetermined learning maps such that each grade level and content area teacher can be observed teaching the same content, in the same way, at the same time.

This rigidity contributes to a cycle of marginalization where lower-performing students get higher levels of structure combined with lower levels of thinking. When we ask students for the one right answer, we fail to ask, "What is the real problem?" or "What are the outcomes of doing it that way?" With lower-level test questions, we fail to expect analysis and original ideas. Imagine that same type of pedantic lesson on the Renaissance being repeated throughout the day as students learn about civics, volume, weather, and characterization. Joseph Simone (2012) explains that

> in education, deficit thinking is the practice of holding lower expectations for students with demographics that do not fit the traditional context of the school system. Deficit thinking equates the poor academic achievement of students from low-income and culturally and linguistically diverse communities with factors outside the control of the school. (p. ii)

Rather than accepting a deficit perspective, Simone advocates for changes in dialogue and practice that spotlight students' assets rather than their deficits.

Instead of focusing on the problems caused by deficit thinking and marginalization, it is time for educators to refocus on the root causes of the problem and on seeking viable solutions. Let's look at the Renaissance lesson through the eyes of the learner. Let's probe the convergence of forces that inspired the Renaissance and compare them to other periods in history. Then support students as they explore an aspect of the period that is of interest to them, such as arts and architecture, explorers, the Gutenberg printing press, or astronomy. All this learning can be synthesized at a Renaissance Faire where each student or group presents their findings on a soapbox or stage. When the requirements for inquiry, content, sequence, and presentation are consistent and clearly explained from the start, students can substantially critique their own and each other's learning outcomes. In doing so, assessment comes to align with the best practices of engaging, informative, flexible, mutual, purposeful, and technically sound. In response, students become reflective and effective managers of their own learning.

REAL ASSESSMENT

In order to get real about assessment, it is essential to return to its roots. Assessment comes from the Latin word *assidere*, meaning to sit beside. When the teacher takes on the role of observer, monitor, and guide of learning, he or she gathers information about students' progress from multiple sources, develops an understanding of what students can do with their knowledge, and uses this information to steer and improve learning.

While there is a wealth of research on best practice in teaching and learning, there is not quite an equivalent amount of information on best practice in assessment. Still, research provides a robust foundation on which to select and construct the best routines in assessment. The underpinnings of quality assessment come from these sources: John Hattie (2011), Robert Marzano (2007), James McMillan (2012), the National Research Council (2001), Linda Darling-Hammond et al. (2013), Dylan Wiliam (2011), and National Center for the Improvement of Educational Assessment (www.nciea.org).

In brief, assessment must include

- coherence with intentional learning outcomes,
- varied methods and pathways,
- participation of the learner,
- focus on growth,
- reciprocity between teacher and student,
- formative processes, and
- responsiveness to evidence of learning.

These are the approaches that are most beneficial for all types of learners.

Some students enter school without having attained the foundations of kindergarten readiness (National Center for Educational Statistics [NCES], 2015). Without these social, emotional, and cognitive skills, over time the learning gaps grow, as does frustration, weariness, and ultimately shutting down and dropping out. When the assessment model is redesigned from one of standardized scores and consequences to a model where all learners can thrive, disenfranchisement is reduced and success becomes more achievable. This means supplanting externally driven measures with local student-focused assessment.

According to Andrade, Huff, and Brooke (2012),

> The broad application of student-centered approaches to learning and assessing has much in common with other education reform movements including closing the achievement gaps and providing equitable access to a high-quality education, especially for underserved youth. (p. 3)

Making assessment inclusive and relevant for dissimilar and disenfranchised learners is the focus of this book. In this way, assessment is returned to its roots of being informative, actionable, and meaningful to both the teacher and the student.

Restorative Assessment

Over the past decades, and even before No Child Left Behind and Every Student Succeeds, too many teachers, students, and schools have been left behind. These policies have moved us too far north of the foundations of assessment and too far south of the principles, purposes, and best practices in assessment. It is time to recenter the compass.

Pixabay

Every teacher and every learner is at risk from testing. Standardized test scores are but one measure in a spectrum of assessments, but they do not provide insight into students' thinking and they do not illuminate gaps during the process of learning. They don't measure essential skills for our students' future such as flexibility, real-world problem solving, and creativity. Noam Chomsky (2015) calls them "artificial." It is local assessment that balances, offsets, and reduces the risks of high-stakes, large-scale standardized tests.

The ideas in this book work because restorative assessment

1. refocuses teaching, learning, and assessing on a broad spectrum of knowledge and skills;

2. reframes the trickle-down approach of curriculum to one that starts with the incoming learner and builds upward from their foundations;

3. incorporates multiple and diverse ways for students to demonstrate learning;

4. delivers information on student learning during learning rather than weeks after it has occurred;

5. provides opportunities for teachers to focus on the needs of their individual students;

6. supports higher-order thinking and deeper levels of learning;

7. reduces the stress of assessment on learners;

8. builds the skills that are most important for student success in the real world; and

9. reinforces the importance of social and emotional skills for lifelong success.

Nurturing a Sustainable Assessment Climate for All Learners

There is no denying that schools have changed. If Rip Van Winkle were to wake up today, he would be astounded by the changes in the world: self-driving cars, electronic personal assistants, global collaboratives, and more. But schools would look more familiar. He would be greeted by a principal and teachers who are on average white females in their 40s (NCES, 2015). In the classroom, he might see a smartboard rather than a blackboard. In some classrooms, students would be seated at desks watching a video or tutorial (rather than listening to a lecture) on King Philip's War.

Today's students would look different to him. Less than half would be white, and the class would include a diverse array of ethnicities, cultures, and nationalities (NCES, 2015). This diversity means that students' experience with language, customs, beliefs, religion, traditions, and views of society also differ. But as the United Nations Educational, Scientific and Cultural Organization (1950) explains, "National, religious, geographic, linguistic and cultural groups do not necessarily coincide with racial groups and are not correlated with learning outcomes" (p. 142).

While diversity informs educational practice, equally, if not more, valuable is the emerging research from the cognitive and behavioral sciences. As children grow and develop, their emotional, social, and intellectual capacities change. As younger children are learning about their world, older ones are preparing to live and work in the real world. While younger ones require tangible examples and concrete applications, the adolescent prefrontal cortex is facilitating analytical thinking and evaluating solutions to problems and outcomes of decisions.

A review by the Center for Public Education (2005) shows that all students can be successful. In schools labeled as *high risk* but consistently demonstrating high levels of performance, multiple indicators were present: high expectations, supported and supportive teachers, community involvement, student engagement in learning, and ongoing diagnostic assessment. This last indicator relied on a comprehensive assessment system that monitored student progress regularly, identified learning challenges, and responded without undue delay. It is this type of internal accountability that is essential to the success of all learners.

This book views assessment comprehensively. This means making it inclusive for all learners while at the same time making it accessible for individual learners. It is built on the belief that in a fair and assessment-rich culture, all students have opportunities to demonstrate continuous progress. You are encouraged to personalize the content and take away what is most relevant locally.

> ## In a schoolwide culture of restorative assessment, these ideals and practices are essential:
>
> - Infusing assessment throughout teaching and learning
>
> - Engaging learners as planners, explorers, and assessors of learning
>
> - Assuming all students are capable of growing the dendrites needed for new learning
>
> - Accepting that mistakes are among the most impactful learning strategies
>
> - Recognizing that mindset and other noncognitive skills strongly influence learning
>
> - Embracing learning and assessment that is meaningful, interesting, real world, and growth-oriented
>
> - Promoting clarity, choice, ownership, and relevance as the foundations of good assessment

Advocating for a focus on assessment rather than testing helps students feel safe in showing their learning and appreciate the value of descriptive feedback. This in turn supports a classroom where they are willing to take reasonable risks and honor growth over final scores. Facilitating this type of change in mindset requires building trust and hopefulness, student by student. To do this, assessment must be transparent and mistakes along the path of learning attentively and reassuringly resolved.

RESPECTING AND VALUING DIVERSITY, INCLUSIVENESS, AND EQUITY

Schools labeled as low performing, high poverty, or turn-around have several characteristics in common including limited resources, non-English speakers, cultural diversity, and family stress. When a discussion about education moves toward the issue of diversity, people respond in disparate ways. Depending on each person's comfort level and knowledge, they may withdraw to a safer topic, approach the topic with apprehension, blame others, or, alternatively, invigorate the conversation with questions and encouragement. Overarching issues in these conversations focus on these key issues:

Diversity: We are all diverse: We live in a global world and in diverse nations. Students entering school in the United States today come from varied cultural and ethnic backgrounds. Living with diversity means accepting and valuing differences rather than shunning them. This is fostered on a foundation of human rights, dignity, and respect for all. We all know someone who is shorter or older than us, wears glasses or uses other adaptive devices, has different political views, prays differently, or has a different level of education. Rather than ignoring differences, use the strengths of diversity in schools to build an inclusive culture of learning and learners.

Equity: This is the foundation of fairness. It means providing students with the opportunities they need to be successful. This is different from equality, which refers to giving all students the same things. Just because I may be overweight does not mean that I eat the same diet as my friend who is the same weight as me. We differ in muscle mass, activity level, and eating pattern. Equity means that I may eat fewer carbs to maintain a similar weight as my friend. This adjustment may lead to our having equal weights. In the classroom, students' inequities may include social, economic, cultural, linguistic, resources, curriculum, instruction, and assessment. Equity can also mean different resources or flexibility in assessment.

Inclusive Pedagogy: Emerging research confirms that among the best assessment practices for all learners are clarity of purpose and outcomes, routinely embedded informative assessment, reciprocal engagement, reflection and self-assessment, meaningful content and contexts, choice in process and product, reasonable challenge, supportive relationships, and a responsive environment.

WHO'S AT RISK?

Students who are at risk of academic difficulties come from all backgrounds. Henri may struggle in math, while Ahmal is challenged by an unfamiliar language. When our eyeglasses are no longer clear or we have a flat tire, we fix it. Fixing doesn't mean that everyone wears the same glasses. It means that some students may need to see the foundations of learning closer to where they are starting out. Others may need to see into the distance and understand how the field in front of them leads to the mountains in the distance.

The class comedian who may be the bane of a teacher's existence may be the next late-night talk show host. The student who spends her time helping others rather than completing her own work may become a community advocate. Oprah was told she wasn't fit for television, Michael Jordan was cut from his high school basketball team, and Albert Einstein didn't talk until he was almost five years old. Eminem, Nelson Mandela, Mahatma Gandhi, Jackie Chan, Ben Carson, and Rosa Parks all overcame poverty, family problems, and discrimination.

Some people are averse to the term *at risk,* believing that it is an overgeneralization of a complex set of factors. Others believe it stigmatizes and labels students who may be less likely to succeed. They prefer to name specific challenges such as culturally diverse, underserved, limited socioeconomic opportunities, behaviorally vulnerable, alienated, academically challenged, developmentally unique, transient, homeless, or experiencing inadequate resources, family breakdown, and hardship.

This book relies on the data that show some groups have a higher risk of academic crumple, breakdown, or collapse. The label doesn't matter. What is important is that changes are made to policy and practice to support all learners. When everyone in a society is productive, the whole society flourishes. When all students have the necessary supports to become successful, the school culture and community thrives. For so many reasons, we are all responsible for lifting up all learners so they can achieve their highest potential. Keep in mind that this potential does not necessarily mean high scores on standardized tests for all, as tests only measure a sliver of what makes people successful.

Whatever term, cause, or descriptor you choose, there are too many students who lack success for numerous reasons. I choose to use the general term at risk throughout this book but also discuss specific challenges these children face. Feel free to rephrase the ideas for your setting.

Jean Ormrod (2006) relies on the research of many to synthesize these ideas when she describes them as "Students who have a high probability of failing to acquire minimal academic skills necessary for success in the adult world" (p. 129). This includes:

Academic Challenges

- Negative school climate, low expectations, lack of appropriate discipline

- Irrelevant and disconnected curriculum

- Unprepared to start school or difficulty completing sequential grade-level work

- Unproductive noncognitive strategies and mindsets

- Grade retention, suspensions, frequent absences, or inability to keep up

Social Circumstances

- Social struggles such as poverty, homelessness, under- or unemployment, and transience

- High-crime neighborhoods

- Family factors such as single-parent household, family instability, and dysfunction

- Misalignment between home and school cultures

- Lack of community services

Student Characteristics

- Personal issues such as behavioral/emotional challenges and mental health issues

- Feeling like they don't belong; not feeling safe

- Low self-efficacy and self-esteem

- Involvement with the legal/justice system

- Speaker of languages other than English

The outcomes for these students are typically poor academic performance, lack of interest in school, misbehavior, truancy, and dropout. "While any one factor—or even several factors—does not necessarily place students at risk, combinations of circumstances identify the potential for failure" (Frymier & Gansneder, 1989, p. 143).

All learners also have different personal characteristics and experiences that can lead to higher or lower levels of success and more or less resiliency. Thus, at risk is a very broad label based on large data sets that are then responded to locally. No child should be summarily labeled as such, but rather, each one needs to be recognized as an individual with unique attributes, requirements, and expectations.

HOW TO RESPOND

Teachers often ask for specific interventions in response to explicit challenges. Keep in mind that

> with the exception of certain characteristics such as learning disabilities, a student's perceived risk status is rarely related to his or her ability to learn or succeed academically, and largely or entirely related to a student's life circumstances. (Glossary of Education Reform, n.d., "At-Risk," para. 3)

This means that each child's needs in relation to specific challenges must be responded to differently. Here are some broad brush strokes to consider and then customize for your setting.

Schoolwide

✓ Connect and engage families in their children's school experiences.

✓ Seek focused and targeted community resources.

✓ Intervene early in emerging problems.

✓ Ensure that every child's physical and safety needs are met.

✓ Support the development of positive relationships with and between peers, groups, schools, and community.

In the Classroom

✓ Strengthen relationships in the classroom: Emphasize the value of compassion, collaboration, and caring.

✓ Make sure learning expectations and processes are clear and attainable.

✓ Model expectations and examples of successful strategies and outcomes.

✓ Deconstruct large ideas and tasks into smaller steps.

✓ Remain consistent and predictable with expectations, rules, and follow-through.

For the Student

✓ Make learning relevant, and personalize as feasible.

✓ Emphasize depth of understanding rather than breadth of content.

✓ Teach success skills such as organization, mindset, and stress management.

✓ Offer encouragement and develop self-esteem while maintaining high expectations.

✓ Provide scaffolds, supports, and interventions within the classroom.

Rather than labeling learners, this book is about making the curriculum relevant, building on students' strengths, setting attainable goals, establishing safe routines, promoting individual mastery, monitoring progress, ensuring necessary supports, incorporating and encouraging higher-level thinking, and engaging learners in learning and the school community.

Of course, there are differences in student performance, just as there are differences between people who are gregarious and those who are shy. Look around your own family and friends. We all perform differently on different tasks. One may be able to fix just about anything, and another may be better at soothing a crying child, yet we continue to compare children on a narrow range of skills measured by large-scale standardized tests. Really knowing what someone knows and can do goes beyond measuring his or her ability to distinguish between metaphor and analogy, or species and genus, or latte and cappuccino.

PATHWAYS TO SUCCESS

We live in a world of soundbites. It is easy to focus on morsels of information to solve life's problems and challenges. It would be easy to believe that "Every cloud has a silver lining," "You can be whatever you want to be," and "Good things come to those who wait." The downside of these platitudes is that they encourage complacency and indifference instead of diligence, determination, and personal responsibility.

Rather than soundbites and platitudes, this book seeks to synthesize the best of what we know about teaching and learning as it relates to the assessment of at-risk populations. It is based on the research and literature on populations who have a higher probability of failure not only in school but also in their lives beyond the schoolhouse.

It is essential to find the hinge point between lock-step standards that all students at every grade level are expected to achieve and excessive personalization that requires a teacher to prepare 30 different instructional routes. Neither are good ideas. A better idea is a shared foundation that supports best practice in teaching and learning in all settings. Each of the chapters discusses the general principles behind the concept and then seeks to address the specific needs of students for whom success is more elusive.

This book is not about extreme makeovers that are hard to sustain or bring to scale. Most districts do not have access to the resources required for a complete school redesign. However, it is possible to borrow the best ideas from these models: Summit Schools, Renaissance Schools, School of the Future, Big Picture Learning, New Tech Network, Expeditionary Learning, and other models. Each has their own unique approach.

Incorporated in their purposeful practice are flexible schedules, individualized plans, diverse pathways to learning, alternative assessment strategies, and the development of noncognitive skills to support student success. These changes can be done with minimal upheaval to existing practice and expense. They must not be viewed as another add-on program that requires extensive implementation and ultimately contributes to initiative fatigue. Rather, it is a set of descriptive guidelines for improving learning outcomes for all students.

Applied Learning

Look through this list of assessment beliefs and practices described in this book. In your professional learning community or individually, select the three to four that are the most important to you. Explain why you chose them and reflect on their relevance to your practice. The numbers reflect the content of each of the chapters in this book. If you find a preponderance of selections from one or two chapters, focus on those as a starting point for personal growth and a teamwork plan.

Central Ideas of This Book

- Assessment is fundamental rather than supplemental to teaching and learning.

- Assessment incorporates a broad spectrum of strategies and outcomes.

- Assessment is an inclusive process: inclusive of all learners and all learning outcomes.

(Continued)

(Continued)

- Assessment is about progress and growth rather than for ranking and comparing.

Ideas and Concepts by Chapter

Chapter 1: Reverting Assessment to Its Intended Purpose

A. Rely on the research on what works best in assessment in learning and assessing.

B. Develop assessment-literate students, teachers, and communities of practice.

C. Recognize that assessment is an informative, mutual, reciprocal, responsive, and inclusive continuous process.

Chapter 2: Restoring Balance

A. Strive for balance between local and large-scale assessment.

B. Seamlessly incorporate multiple strategies and measures.

C. Assess throughout the levels of the taxonomy.

Chapter 3: Reinstating Mastery and Growth

A. Emphasize the process rather than products of teaching and learning.

B. Spotlight mastery and utilize growth measures to illuminate assets and fortify weak spots.

C. Embed practical and relevant formative assessment throughout teaching and learning.

Chapter 4: Refocusing on Learners

A. Foster and facilitate assessment-capable learners who are goal setters and monitors of learning.

B. Strengthen, encourage, and engage learners as self-assessors.

C. Utilize multiple pathways to further personalization, flexibility, choice, and voice.

Chapter 5: Reconsidering Noncognitive Skills and Attributes

A. Stretch beyond cognitive skills: Assess the proficiencies for success.

B. Noncognitive attributes are essential to the success of all learners.

C. Weave assessment within teaching and learning.

Which ideas are most important to me and/or my team? What are the priorities?

1. _____

2. _____

3. _____

4. _____

What questions do I/we have and what do I/we want to learn more about?

1. _____

2. _____

3. _____

4. _____

CHAPTER 1

Reverting Assessment to Its Intended Purpose

Chapter Goals/Key Ideas
Assessment literacy is the foundation of sound and sensible practice. *A synthesis of rigorous research reveals the MUSTs of quality assessment.* *Assessment is a continuously engaging, illuminating, and reciprocal process.* *Flexibility, inclusion, and responsiveness are essential elements of restorative assessment.* *Assessment is at its best when it is technically sound, valid, fair, and equitable.*

ASSESSMENT MATTERS

For many students, and adults too, the word *assessment* can activate images of difficult tests and feelings of anxiety. But that is not its intent. In translation, assessment originates from the Latin word *assidere,* meaning to sit beside. When teachers and students sit beside each other, they review and respond to the progress and outcomes of learning. These responses may identify gaps in understanding, inform instructional practices, decide on alternative resources, guide next steps, motivate and engage students. In essence, assessment is intended to be a mutual and informative process.

Over time, assessment came to denote a fixed amount of tax or fine. This later morphed into an estimate of the value of property that ultimately determined a property owner's tax base. Compare this to the word *examination* that is derived from the Latin *examinare,* meaning to weigh, test, or judge. While examination remains similar to its original intent, assessment has moved far off its intended purpose. With new policy and emerging insights from the learning sciences, this is an ideal time to return assessment to its original meaning.

Measurement gives learning a number. For example, the number 10 means nothing when taken out of context. It can mean you are in tenth place or have a golf handicap of 10. *Evaluation* provides a comparative value to the number. Until we know the total number, mean, or "cut score," we don't know what it represents: Is it below the acceptable median or mean? Does it signify overall satisfactory achievement or excellence in just one skill?

Before moving into a deeper understanding of assessment, it is also important to recognize that a *test* is simply a strategy. Learners can be tested with selected-choice questions, an essay, or a problem to solve. When we use the student's answers to measure learning and compare them to others in the group, we are evaluating. It is not until we use the information about the student's knowledge and skills to inform decisions and improve learning outcomes that the strategy becomes an assessment. Yet in education, we continue to label exams as *assessments*, and standardized tests as *instructive*.

The thermometer (the test) may read 68 degrees Fahrenheit (the data), and one person in the room may say he or she is cold and another complains that it is too hot (evaluation). It is when they decide whether to adjust the thermostat, or for one to take off a sweatshirt, or for the other to curl up with a blanket, that assessment takes place. It is assessment that makes learning visible, analyzes instructional effectiveness, and informs instructional decisions.

Consider these three descriptions of assessment:

1. "Assessment is the process of gathering and discussing information from multiple and diverse sources in order to develop a deep understanding of what students know, understand, and can do with their knowledge as a result of their educational experiences; the process culminates when assessment results are used to improve subsequent learning" (Huba and Freed, 2000, p. 8).

2. It is insufficient simply to point out right and wrong answers to students. For assessment to be effective, a student must

    - come to hold a concept of quality roughly similar to that of the teacher,

    - be able to compare the current level of performance with the standard, and

    - be able to take action to close the gap.

The teacher's role is to help the student internalize quality criteria by translating them "from latent to manifest and back to latent again" until these criteria become "so obviously taken for granted that they need no longer be stated explicitly" (Sadler, 1989, p.73).

3. The research indicates that improving learning through assessment depends on deceptively simple key factors:

   - The active involvement of pupils in their own learning;

   - Adjusting teaching to take account of the results of assessment;

   - A recognition of the profound influence assessment has on the motivation and self-esteem of pupils, both of which are crucial influences on learning;

   - The need for pupils to be able to assess themselves and understand how to improve (Black & Wiliam 1998a p. 2).

In what ways are they alike and different?

Alike: _____

Different _____

Which is closest to your beliefs? Why? ____
_____

Trudy Banta and Catherine Palomba (1999) encapsulate these core ideas when they explain that "assessment is the systematic collection, review, and use of information about educational programs undertaken for the purpose of improving student learning and development" (p. 4).

To Summarize: Assessment includes all the actions of teachers, students, districts, and states that involve gathering and analyzing information about performance that is used for the improvement of teaching and learning. It is this process of obtaining information that identifies strengths, weaknesses, and lingering gaps; informs decisions about students; provides feedback about progress; and judges instructional effectiveness. Assessment is fundamentally about the outcomes of teaching and learning.

An instructional strategy that is helpful in understanding the complexities of written text relies on converting text to visual word clouds. By entering each descriptive word as many times as it is written in the document, the most common terms emerge as larger text. Using Tagxedo or Wordle, key vocabulary is visually displayed as shown in the image below. In doing so, complex texts are simplified so that the reader can focus on the important ideas rather than wading through a sea of words. This also provides an opportunity to decode the vocabulary and construct understanding. In this example, the key words are: strengths, weaknesses, criteria, gather, respond, action, and adjust.

Wordle.com

KEY IDEAS AND PURPOSES OF ASSESSMENT

Most educators recognize these essential elements of assessment. However,

> while assessment has the potential to improve learning for all students, historically it has acted as a barrier rather than a bridge to educational opportunity. Assessments have been used to label students and put them in dead-end tracks. (Dietel, Herman, & Knuth, 1991, p. 5)

Assessment has been deconstructed, explained, and demonstrated by people with deep expertise on the topic, yet testing continues to lead the conversation about educational assessment. As Linda Darling-Hammond (2016) points out, "We are using the wrong kinds of tests in the wrong kinds of ways."

Assessment must be restored to its original purposes, especially for students who experience academic, personal, social, and economic obstacles. Assessment that makes a difference for all learners

1. aligns with desired learning outcomes,

2. is an integral element of teaching and learning rather than an add-on,

3. continuously gathers information about learning,

4. relies on strategies that are transparent to the learner from the start,

5. helps students set learning goals and the means for achieving them,

6. provides multiple opportunities for students to demonstrate proficiency,

7. illuminates student knowledge and understanding,

8. identifies students' educational needs,

9. informs next steps for the teacher and the student,

10. supports and encourages higher levels of thinking,

11. guides curriculum design and modification, and

12. provides feedback about learning to multiple constituents.

In other words, assessment must be flexible, enabling all students to demonstrate skills and knowledge in relevant ways. Meaningful assessment considers their incoming knowledge, life experiences, and worldview. It takes into account incoming inequalities. These fundamental ideas for turning research into practice are worth exploring more deeply.

Reflection

Consider the list of the purposes of assessment. Which three matter the most to you and your students? Why? Compare your list to your colleagues and collectively develop a list of priorities.

1.

2.

3.

ASSESSMENT LITERACY

Assessment literacy requires a comprehensive approach to measuring learning—from prior learning to final outcomes and next steps. The most effective teachers know what their students need to learn and regularly monitor that learning.

Standardized tests measure and report only a small portion of the full curriculum. The balance is left to teachers in the classroom. Thus, they must be proficient in basic assessment skills and knowledge. Every day, they connect students, pedagogy, and measurement as they routinely integrate big-picture standards with the assessment of individual learning outcomes. Norman Webb (2002) explains that

> Assessment Literate teachers possess the knowledge about how to assess what students know and can do, interpret the results of these assessments, and apply these results to improve student learning and program effectiveness. (p. 3)

Organizations with standards for teachers' assessment literacy include

- Council for the Accreditation of Educator Preparation (formerly NCATE),

- Council of Chief State School Officers, and

- National Board for Professional Teaching Standards.

In addition, each state has its own credentialing standards. These standards recognize the underlying foundations of assessment literacy and the design of meaningful assessments. Consistent across sources are the following fundamental ideas.

CLARITY OF PURPOSE

- Multiple measures are used to inform growth and mastery.

- Content, instruction, environment, and student attributes all guide assessment practice.

- Alignment between instruction and assessment is robust.

- Assessments are planned for appropriate, specific, and visible purposes.

- Teachers are knowledgeable about and use different types of assessment, from selected choice to precision rubrics.

PROCESS

- Reliable, consistent, and compelling research informs practice.

- Large-scale standards are unpacked, resulting in assessable portions of content.

- Teachers create/select high-quality local assessments.

- Student learning is continuously monitored.

- Learners are engaged as goal setters and self-assessors.

- Teachers comprehend and appreciate the technical elements of assessment.

OUTCOME/RESPONSE

- Teachers plan, differentiate, and modify instruction based on assessment data.

- Teachers and students work toward closing gaps between performance and capability.

- Assessment results are analyzed and used to improve teaching and learning.

- Professional growth and support is ongoing.

- Outcomes are effectively communicated to multiple audiences and users of information.

Assembling the building blocks of assessment literacy results in the grid shown in Table 1.1 that displays the properties, elements, and attributes of assessment literacy. Keep in mind that this is not a linear process but rather can take varying pathways in order to make distinct connections.

TABLE 1.1   Elements and Attributes of Assessment Literacy

FOUNDATIONS	PURPOSE: Rationale for Assessment	PROCESS: Development of Insight	OUTCOMES: Results Inform Response
TEACHING	Inform Pedagogy	Learning Outcomes	Response
TIMING	Before Teaching	During Learning	After Instruction
FUNCTION	Diagnostic	Formative	Summative

EXAMPLES

Recall and Understanding

Learning Intention: Explain how a character's actions contributed to the sequence of events.

Pedagogy/Process: Diagnostic, During Learning.

Outcome/Analysis: In the story of the turtle and the hare, why did the hare lose the race?

1. He ran too slowly.
2. He stopped to eat lunch.
3. He knew he was ahead so he took a nap.
4. His sneakers weren't very good.

Learning Intention: Adding and subtracting within 1,000.

Pedagogy/Process: Formative, Before Teaching.

Outcome: Solve a subtraction problem using a number line.

Higher and Deeper Thinking

Learning Intention: Use textual evidence to support analysis.

Process: After Instruction, Higher and Deeper Outcomes (analyze, investigate, compare).

Analysis of Learning Outcomes: "We eat what we are." Explain that quote by comparing eating patterns around the world as influenced by climate, culture, technology, and economics.

Learning Intention: Complete a multistep task. Explain your actions and learning to another.

Process: Graphically illustrate the steps for finding a book in the library.

Outcome: Turn your steps into advice for Shalicia to find a book on medieval feminist literature or the first humans in the Western Hemisphere. If she is unable to find a book, suggest search words for an online search. Explain your choice of words.

IN PRACTICE

Ms. Lee wants to use assessment to support her planned instruction (pedagogy) during learning, in a formative way, as students deepen their thinking about the rights and responsibilities of free speech. Together, her class scrutinizes and analyzes the First Amendment. Small groups each read or view additional information and/or case studies to develop deeper understanding. The whole class reviews examples of speech that is protected and speech that is not protected by the Constitution. During this exercise, students reflect and summarize their own thinking about the speech, compare it to the class analysis, and note lingering questions. Then, individually or with a partner, they present a short speech or brief case study and ask the class to determine whether it is protected or not. They use a scorecard to record the results. In doing so, Ms. Lee has combined the purpose of diagnosing learning with a formative process that supports and assesses higher and deeper learning.

1. Give Ms. Lee advice on an assessment strategy that would reveal her students' depth of understanding.

2. What do you suggest she do if she notes that some students have not moved their meter and still believe they can say anything they want, to or about anyone, at any time, through any communication channel?

Discussion Points

1. Why is it important for teachers to be assessment literate?

2. What challenges do teachers face in meeting assessment literacy standards?

3. How does this differ for high-risk students? Consider their unique academic needs, social, cultural, or interpersonal uniqueness.

4. Based on assessment literacy standards:

    a. Which aspects do you feel comfortable with?

    b. Which elements do you want to improve?

5. Give an example of how you will connect the elements of assessment literacy.

RESEARCH-BASED BEST PRACTICES IN ASSESSMENT

When research-based practices are utilized throughout teaching, learning, and assessing, the risk of failure is reduced and opportunities for success are increased. These best practices are fundamental to the achievement of all students. But for students who are marginalized because of poverty, cultural differences, behavioral regulation, stress, and more, these routines are especially important. Students are most successful when they feel they are swimming with rather than against the stream; when they know where the stream is headed and that there will be guidance, scaffolds, and ladders along the journey; and that they can travel at their own pace and will ultimately arrive at their destination.

> High-quality assessment provides education stakeholders—from state officials to teachers and principals, to students and parents—with the necessary information to adapt the learning process at various levels to meet the needs of each and every student. (Northwest Evaluation Association, 2016, p. 8)

There are numerous studies illuminating what best practice means in classroom assessment. Researchers and practitioners including John Hattie, James McMillan, Robert Marzano, Dylan Wiliam, Paul Black, Terry Crooks, Margaret Heritage, Heidi Andrade, Linda Darling-Hammond, Susan Brookhart, and James Pellegrino are but a few whose insights and analyses are routinely relied on. A synthesis of research results in the acronym MUST that stands for Mutual, Useful, Supportive, and Technically Sound. Table 1.2 provides a brief summary of those ideas. Throughout the book, selected ideas will be emphasized as they explicitly align and support restorative assessment.

TABLE 1.2   The MUSTs of Assessment

1. *ASSESSMENT IS **MUTUAL**: Reciprocal, Aligned, Visible, Illuminating, Responsive*
A. Systemically *aligned* with standards, curriculum, teaching, learning, and assessment
B. *Purposefully planned* to support and improve teaching and learning
C. Learning intentions, assessment strategies, and specifications for scoring and evaluating are *clear and evident*
D. Mutual assessment *monitors progress*: Teaching is *responsive* to learning and lingering gaps.
2. *ASSESSMENT IS **USEFUL**: Informative, Motivational, Embedded, Growth Oriented*
A. Clear assessment criteria support and engage *learners as assessors* and goal setters
B. Students recognize *strategies for achieving and assessing* outcomes: Learning is supported with exemplars and guidance.
C. Assessment is *interwoven throughout teaching and learning* in order to continuously gather "data."
D. Emphasis is on a cycle of *growth and improvement*. Opportunities for improvement are provided. Growth toward mastery over time guides instructional decisions.

3. **ASSESSMENT IS _STICKY_**: _Supportive, Engaging, Real World, Flexible, Student Focused_

   A. Students have _choices_, in both process and product, for showing what they know and can do.

   B. _Real-world challenges_ raise attention to task: Interest-based strategies sustain _higher and deeper_ learning.

   C. _Multiple measures_ are used to assess multiple types, levels, and depths of learning.

   D. _Formative strategies and feedback_ are responsive and emphasize individual strengths and strategies for overcoming challenges.

4. **ASSESSMENT IS _TECHNICALLY SOUND_**: _Valid, Reliable, Fair, Balanced_

   A. Assessments are _valid_, meaning they measure the intended outcomes and inferences made from them are accurate. Adequately samples students' knowledge, understanding, and skills.

   B. Assessments are _reliable_, meaning they are consistent across groups, place, and time

   C. Assessments are _fair_, meaning they are free from bias, inequity, and stereotype.

   D. _Varied strategies serving multiple purposes_ (informative, diagnostic, and summative) are used to elicit objective evidence of learning.

When visitors, coaches, or supervisors walk into two different classrooms in the same school, it is not uncommon for assessments to look different. In one class, students are bent over paper or screens completing selected-choice questions such as:

Thomas Jefferson opposed a National Bank because:

A. It was too risky

B. It would cost too much

C. It was unconstitutional

D. It took power away from the states

In another, there is excitement as students present their support of Alexander Hamilton's advocacy for a strong central government versus Thomas Jefferson's ideas on decentralization. Students listen to the fact-supported arguments and then peer assess the content and use on valid source materials, as well as the quality of the presentation (clarity, logical sequence, etc.). Then, as an assessment, students cast and defend their vote for their choice of government based on the evidence and arguments.

When students are engaged in assessment, the focus changes from a comparative and competitive nature to one of growth and improvement. While the discussion over federalists and republicans in this classroom spurred contentious discussion, it was done in an atmosphere of exuberant learning and courteous debate.

It was easy and expedient in the first classroom for the first teacher to use questions from a test bank. But it also meant taking the time to verify that instruction was closely aligned with the test-based questions. Alternative types of assessment also take time and effort on the part of the teacher but are better able to incorporate the best practices of engagement, flexibility, and inclusiveness of all learners. In the second classroom, the teacher put many elements in place to guide students toward success, including clear expectations and learning outcomes, a structured process that also provided flexibility, and an atmosphere of mutuality with an emphasis on growth.

Some of the best practices in Table 1.2 are explored in this chapter—specifically, the ideas of mutual, responsive, reciprocal, inclusive, and technically sound. You will find others such as multiple measures in Chapter 2, growth and improvement in Chapter 3, and choice and engagement in Chapter 4 as they relate to at-risk learners.

MUTUAL

Learning is by nature a mutual process. Imagine learning to play golf or mastering a new language without any help. Independent trial and error may work for a few people, but typically, learning outcomes are better when they rely on guidance, support, and gauges of progress. Rather than a sage on the stage, a teacher is more like a symphony conductor, helping students master their instruments and learning to play together as each works toward a consistent production of volume, tone, and tempo.

In the classroom, mutuality means cooperatively recognizing strengths and responding to gaps in learning. This is rooted in respect and trust. It isn't always easy when students live in a stressful environment where it may be difficult to depend on others to provide care and meet their basic needs. Mutual accountability also begins with small steps. When a teacher says he or she will bring graph paper tomorrow and the student says he or she will return a library book tomorrow, and they both act on their word, mutuality and trust will then develop.

Teachers earn students' trust step by step and day by day. It begins by listening deeply to students rather than "I hear you" type of listening. It also means offering an empathetic response such as, "I understand why you are so frustrated." When a teacher validates a student's feelings, yet also anticipates a positive resolution, he or she is sharing a message of optimism about the outcomes. This in turn facilitates a problem-solving process that deeply explores the causes of a problem and seeks potential solutions. As responsibility is gradually released to students, they begin to see opportunities for independently achieving better outcomes. Mutuality starts with meeting simple needs and expectations and develops into a willingness to try new things and take academic risks.

In general, younger children are more trusting of adults, but after years of behavioral mandates, consequences, and failure, adolescents may forget that they have the ability to be curious and confident learners. Trust is a two-way street for the adults too. When teachers are repeatedly reprimanded for not raising test scores or not keeping students in their seats, over time, they too are less willing to allow students to set individual goals and work independently.

Mutuality and trust are based on these components (synthesized from Brewster & Railsback, 2003; Rimm-Kaufman & Sandilos, 2011; and Tschannen-Moran, 2014):

- Compassion: A sense that the other person has your best interests at heart and cares about you.

- Consistency: Feeling that the person will be available and will follow through as needed.

- Capability/Credibility: Has the expertise to perform the tasks required by his or her role.

- Integrity: The person is truthful and follows through on his or her words.

- Nonjudgmental: Acknowledges and accepts the emotions, beliefs, and the baggage each of us carries.

- Acceptance: Takes students seriously; believes in their potential.

- Interest: Attentive to the student. Accepts disclosures at his or her level of comfort.

- Reciprocity: Shares a sense of mutuality, that we are learning together.

- Openness and Authenticity: Recognizes the teacher and others as having feelings and shortcomings.

- Fairness: Believes that expectations are clear, consistent, and fair for all.

Trust and mutuality are supported by clear success criteria and achievable pathways for success. When students know the starting point as well as the destination, they are better able to monitor their steps along the way. When guardrails and scaffolds are available, they know they can grasp a handrail when they need help. They also know that someone is watching out for them and has their back as they begin to falter.

Reflection/Application

1. What steps do you take to help students feel that learning is a mutual activity and your classroom is a safe place to learn?

2. What would you like to modify about your practice?

RECIPROCAL

Socrates, an early adopter of reciprocity in assessment, guided students in their thinking and deeply questioned their ideas. He provoked students when they were unclear, encouraged them to elaborate on their thinking, and circulated questions between students.

RESTORATIVE ASSESSMENT

"EDUCATION IS THE KINDLING OF A FLAME, NOT THE FILLING OF A VESSEL."

— SOCRATES

Image Source: https://creativecommons.org/licenses/by/2.5/deed.en (CC BY 2.5) Photographer: Marie-Lan Nguyen

Turning the theories that support best practice into action requires deconstructing the essential elements, ensuring that learning intentions are clear, pathways to success are evident, and measures of learning are flexible rather than rigid. In doing so, the hopelessness of traditional measures is softened for students who are at greater risk of failure. In other words, assessment needs to more closely align with Socratic methods than with standardized tests.

Assessment, at its core, is a reciprocal and shared process. This means that teachers are engaged with students during assessment and also engage learners in assessing. All learners must have opportunities and supports necessary for success, including

1. well-defined, visible, and attainable learning outcomes;

2. assessment methods that are known from the start;

3. active involvement in learning and assessing;

4. varied and flexible pathways for achievement; and

5. multiple opportunities for demonstrating learning.

In a restorative classroom, building trust is a reciprocal process that is embedded throughout teaching and learning. It is based on a safe and well-managed classroom environment, focuses on consistency and fairness, relies on reasonable rules and routines, emphasizes empathy and the value of walking in someone else's shoes, and being ready to wipe the slate clean.

IN PRACTICE

1. Invite students to solve a problem you are having with the class such as chronic lateness, excessive chattiness, incomplete assignments, and distracting others. Teach them how to utilize a structured problem-solving process as they analyze

each step and propose feasible solutions. When everyone feels they have contributed to the resolution of the problem, they are more apt to abide by it. This is not unlike teachers who are given a new set of assessments each year. They are more apt to implement them with integrity and consistency if they feel they have contributed to their selection.

2. Place less significance on high-stakes selected-choice tests and more on alternative measures. When students are learning about photosynthesis, rather than asking questions about the sequence, ask them to illustrate what could happen at each stage if the natural sequence is not followed. Instead of selected-choice questions, provide opportunities for them to annotate completion questions, for example: "I am sure of this answer because ___"; or "There may be two answers to this"; or "I know we read about this, and I can't remember that one answer, but here is what I do recall." The mistaken idea of testing is that motivating students by competition not only undermines trust, it encourages students to try to outdo others instead of actually learning together. Further, it incites base instincts of aggression, dominance (like bullying), and unethical behavior such as cheating.

3. Provide increasingly complex opportunities for students to take ownership of assessing their learning. If they are working in a group where each individual has personal responsibility for contributing, use a chart to record: who began the assignment, who suggested solutions, who clarified ideas, who facilitated and monitored the discussion, who recorded the learning, what role did each person take in contributing to the final outcome, decision, or product?

Reflection/Application

1. What strategies can you use at the start of the school year to develop an understanding of mutuality, responsiveness, and reciprocity in your students?

2. How will you build trust with and among students?

3. What will you do to help students understand that teaching and learning is a reciprocal process?

4. What steps will you take during the year to make assessment a mutual and responsive process?

RESPONSIVE

Synchrony between people who don't know each other takes dedication and perseverance. In the classroom, the goal is to build a sense of cohesion and community. Unity and cohesiveness begin on the first day of school and continue throughout the year. One strategy is to begin by seeking commonalities in students' lives. Even when children are diverse, they will find that they have family celebrations, family members who seem to hold everyone together, shared experiences of laughter and sadness, and family maxims to live by.

Traditional activities at the start of the school year include sharing of interests, discussion of stories or posters explaining why and how the classroom is a judgment-free zone, and collaborative development of rules. In a restorative classroom, trust building is an important part of emotional well-being. Abraham Maslow (1943), in his Hierarchy of Needs, identified safety as the foundation for survival and growth. For some students, this means the availability of adequate food and safe water. Once physiological needs are met, a sense of psychosocial safety is equally essential.

One way to begin is to discuss what makes students feel safe at school and ready to learn. Sasha says she doesn't like to be yelled at, and Ramon wants to know that it is okay to sometimes forget things. Use sticky notes or Padlet to share, sort, and identify similarities and differences. Then extend these ideas to collaboratively develop classroom guidelines for success. This turns the broad brushstroke of trust and respect into a reciprocal and personal dialogue about responsibility.

Follow through on these foundations throughout teaching and learning. Make sure that expectations, both learning and behavioral, are clear and achievable. Use formative feedback to make praise specific to the behavior, for example, "The way you reiterated and responded to Jamal's answer helped him feel validated." Take conversations about the lack of compliance outside the classroom.

INCLUSIVE

In their draft standards, the Joint Committee on Standards for Educational Evaluation (2015) state that

> classroom assessment practices meet the standards of quality when teachers are confident that their assessment practices provide accurate and dependable information about students' learning, are free of bias, and are inclusive of all students. (pp. 4, 22)

Assessment was never intended to exclude certain students, nor was it meant to be a bragging club for high scorers. It was meant for growth.

Inclusiveness incorporates several indicators of best practice in assessment. As discussed previously, mutuality is important. In addition, responsiveness, respectfulness, and personalization are significant elements. Pane, Steiner, Baird, and Hamilton (2015) report that "The longer students personalize learning practices, the greater their growth in achievement" (p. 8).

Strategies for strengthening inclusive assessment in a restorative classroom:

1. Maintain consistent standards while offering varied, modified, and tailored pathways for learning and assessing.

2. Rely on differentiation in both learning and assessing: As needed, simplify language, shorten steps, and provide visual cues.

3. Provide multiple ways for students to demonstrate emerging competencies as they progress toward mastery, such as learning logs and self-reflection.

4. Incorporate regular formative assessment in order to identify misunderstanding, and respond appropriately. Consider using structured graphic organizers or sure/not sure charts.

5. Be sensitive to biases and stereotypes in externally provided and teacher- and student-developed assessments. Simplify complex words such as *cognizant* to *aware*, and *proximity* to *near*. Avoid slang, acronyms, and cultural and regional dialects—for example, *water fountain* and *bubbler*.

6. Track progress as well as growth rather than solely summative scores. Support students with learning trackers with apps and programs such as Formative or Quia.

Inclusiveness is essential in restorative classrooms where the classroom atmosphere is as important as the pedagogy. When a student has a sense of emotional well-being, he or she is more willing to engage in learning. When a classroom is mutual and supportive, students are more likely to be successful. Starting each day with a tradition such as a class-developed motto that starts with "I can . . . and I will . . ." or having students create a personalized success anagram gives each individual an opportunity to personalize his or her learning and approach assessment with an open mind and can-do attitude. Morning meetings with a specific purpose each day can be used at all grade levels. For example: "If you had any superpower, what would it be?" or "How can we solve this problem in our room?" Alternatively, use a topic related to the day's learning, such as, "If you could go to any planet, what would it be and why?"

Classroom Success Anagram

S = Set specific and achievable goals

U = Understand and rely on your personal strengths

C = Confer, collaborate, and cooperate with others to improve your quality of work

C = Commit to doing your best work; chip away at it step by step; celebrate success

E = Engage in the experience; embrace the challenge

S = Stay focused on the task at hand

S = Strategy can help you achieve your purpose

Ramonda's Individual Success Anagram

I will overcome ob**S**tacles

I can s**U**cceed, but I'll do it my way

Keep **C**alm and try a different way

There's no fast track to suc**C**ess, you have to take the stairs

My **E**xperience helps me learn

Mi**S**takes are the roller coaster of learning

If you want to reach for the **S**tars, start with a plan

Explicitly teaching reflective listening also builds feelings of understanding and inclusion. In reflective classroom discussions, students are expected to respond with a statement that first summarizes/acknowledges the prior speaker's ideas or feelings and then respectfully adds their own ideas. Many of the best practices in assessment rely on inclusiveness: transparency, choice, embedded assessment, real-world connections, monitoring progress, multiple methods, and meaningful engagement.

Reflection

1. What benefits are there of inclusive assessment?

2. What can teachers do to ensure that all students feel welcome, comfortable, valued, and involved in learning and assessing?

3. What elements of inclusive assessment do you want to blend into your own teaching and learning? What are your first steps?

Reflection: Individually or in your professional learning community (PLC), add more ideas to the list of inclusive strategies.

CASE STUDIES IN INCLUSIVE ASSESSMENT

Read the scenarios and then individually or with your PLC consider how you would respond to one or both of these teachers. Give him or her three specific steps to take to provide both insight and skill-building.

Manuelo, an experienced and capable teacher, is concerned that he is not reaching all the students in his class. He has never before had this range of diversity—from students who don't speak English to those who bring serious family problems and excessive personal baggage to school every day. The ability range is also more wide ranging than ever, and the students seem more bogged down with personal problems than in the past. He is having trouble connecting with his students, prioritizing and responding to their problems, and building relationships with them.

1.

2.

3.

You are mentoring Tabithia, a new teacher in your culturally and academically diverse school. She comes to you after the first two weeks of school dismayed at the wide range of scores on her students' preassessment of knowledge and skills. In some cases, these differences are three to four grade levels apart. At the same time, she has been handed the school's curriculum with a map and timetable. Her stress levels have been raised, and she doesn't know where to begin.

1.

2.

3.

TECHNICALLY SOUND ASSESSMENT

Assessment is only purposeful as far as it honors and sustains precision and accuracy. There is little purpose in assessing what hasn't yet been taught (for example, using a new technology) or assessing under stressful situations (such as, the roof is leaking). Technically sound assessments are constructed on three essential elements: validity, reliability, and fairness.

VALID AND RELIABLE

Validity refers to how well the assessment is measuring what it intends to measure. This refers to precision in both the content being assessed and the construction of the questions. Also, they align with targeted levels of the taxonomy. An important aspect of validity is the accuracy of the interpretations and inferences that are being made about teachers and students. It is essential that decisions and actions taken in response to the assessment are appropriate and precise.

Validity is higher when there is one correct answer that aligns with what was specifically taught. This works well when questions measure only one construct based on explicit instruction. It is more difficult to ensure validity with projects that require higher levels of thinking. This may be due to different instructional strategies and assessment methods among teachers in the same grade level or content area. Validity may also be reduced when there are only one or two questions measuring each of the identified learning outcomes, thus not providing enough data on which to make accurate decisions. Standardized tests claim to be more valid, but that is only if the requisite knowledge was explicitly taught in the same way to every student in the classroom or, alternatively, if the construct was measured multiple times in different ways. Validity may be reduced by stress, ineffective accommodations, and uncomfortable testing environments.

Reliability means the results are consistent across teachers, students, and classrooms, even when students are assessed with different types of measures, (such as, multiple choice versus. a lab experiment). Assessment is most reliable when teachers teach from the same curriculum in the same way and when tests are administered under the same controlled conditions in relation to location, environment, and time. When assessment results are reliable, the outcomes are generalizable to similar populations. Alternative types of assessment can be made more valid when teachers in different classrooms share specific learning outcomes, give the assessments under the same circumstances such as time of day, and share common scoring criteria.

Diverse Views on Validity and Reliability

Aaron Churchill (2015) believes that standardized tests are effective measures of learning because they objectively measure common standards, support accurate comparisons between teachers, schools, and states, and hold them accountable for test outcomes.

Alternatively, James Popham (1999) states that

> standardized achievement tests should not be used to judge the quality of education. Students' scores on these tests do not provide an accurate index of educational effectiveness in that any inference about educational quality made on the basis of students' standardized achievement test performances is apt to be invalid. (p. 9)

In this released third-grade PARCC test, a wrong answer may mean that either the student didn't understand the text or didn't have adequate vocabulary knowledge.

What does the phrase his teeth jiggled show about Pinkerton?

A. He feels pain

B. He feels weary

C. He feels eager

D. He feels nervous

In this algebra question, it is difficult to tell whether a student didn't understand the mathematical concept or the wording of the question.

At the beginning of an experiment, the number of bacteria in a colony was counted at time $t = 0$. The number of bacteria in the colony at "t" minutes after the initial count is modeled by the function $b(t) = 4(2)^t$.

Which value and unit represent the average rate of change in the number of bacteria for the first 5 minutes of the experiment? Select all that apply.

A. 24   B. 24.8   C. 25.4   D. 25.6

E. bacteria   F. minutes   G. bacteria per minute   H. minutes per bacteria

Restorative Validity and Reliability

In a restorative classroom, there are strategies that support authenticity, innovation, and flexibility in assessment while also maintaining validity and reliability. Here are some suggestions:

1. Include the previously stated learning intentions(s) with each task or question.

2. Use a similar verb in the question as in the learning outcome. For example, if the learning outcome requires a student to describe something, then an aligned question may ask a student to identify or explain it rather than analyze it.

3. Offer students a choice in responding. For some, T/F or

multiple choice is more exacting, while others prefer to write in their answer along with an explanation of their thinking.

4. Encourage students to annotate their test with comments such as: "During class we talked about this topic in relation to ___ so I'm not sure how it relates to ___, but _____ seems to be the best answer, although ___ also seems relevant because ___.

5. Offer students a choice in showing what they know. Be sure the same learning outcomes are being measured with each strategy. For understanding the sequence of a story, students could create a timeline using Timetoast or a rap song that they record with Vocaroo or Audacity.

In Your Learning Community:

Reflection

Discuss the pros and cons of various types of assessment, such as selected choice, completion, essay, performance, portfolios, and projects.

Application

1. Select one assessment you are required to give your students.

2. Analyze the validity and reliability of the assessment.

3. Discuss steps that you can take to ensure that assessments are valid and reliable.

FAIR AND EQUITABLE

Fair means unbiased for all learners and inclusive of all ethnicities, cultures, nationalities, races, socioeconomic groups, physicality, and genders. Fairness means all students have appropriate opportunities to achieve learning outcomes. For example, is a test based on solving mathematical word problems assessing mathematical abilities or understanding of language? Most large-scale standardized tests have been validated in relation to the learning intentions. However, some inadvertently require prior knowledge or experience with specific materials. Asking the student about bicycling may also require an understanding of gears. Another student may rely on his or her personal eating experiences when describing or analyzing a healthy meal.

Views From the Experts

Gordon Stobart (2005) believes "that fairness is fundamentally a sociocultural, rather than a technical issue and that fair assessment cannot be considered in isolation from both the curriculum and the educational opportunities" (p. 275). His recommendations for ensuring fairness include:

1. Assessment methods that respect beliefs, inclinations, or needs of certain groups or individuals. This means not requiring all learners to complete a technology-based assessment with a group of diverse students.

2. Consider whether the form and content of the assessment is appropriate for all learners.

3. Check that knowledge and skills are not specific to a cultural group.

4. Be sensitive to linguistic diversity even among learners from a similar culture.

5. Remove metaphors, comparisons, and symbols that may be historically or culturally based.

Linda Suskie (2000) also urges teachers to be fair and equitable in assessing.

If we are to draw reasonably good conclusions about what our students have learned, it is imperative that we make our assessments—and our uses of the results—as fair as possible for as many students as possible. (p. 1)

Her recommendations include the following:

1. Assessment must align with visible learning outcomes that are understood by students.

2. Assessments must match what has been taught.

3. Multiple kinds of measures are considered when making decisions.

4. Consider growth, not solely final scores.

5. Evaluate, reflect, and modify assessments when results don't align with expected outcomes.

Restoring Fairness

To these ideas, I would add:

1. Provide students with opportunities to explain their answer or describe why they are grappling with a question.

2. Be sure students have opportunities to show what they have learned in different ways. One may produce a PowToon, while another writes a letter to the editor.

3. Before turning in their tests, students can post the two most difficult or confusing questions. A pattern will often emerge once all have posted. In response, a brief reteach can reduce uncertainties before the students submit their tests.

4. Embed assessment throughout learning in order to immediately guide interventions and respond to misconceptions.

Equity Versus Equality

An important component of fairness is *equity*, often described as just, reasonable, and unbiased. Blankenship, Noguera, and Kelly (2016) describe it as "A commitment to ensure that every student receives what he or she needs to succeed" (p. 8). Equity is influenced by policy and budgets that may be more difficult to change due to economic and political factors. On the other hand, practice is more malleable. It is possible to change the assessment opportunities that students need to succeed. And these can be changed at the student and classroom level rather than waiting for policy and politics to lead the way.

Inequities in Assessment

- At present, every student in the United States, with few exceptions, is required to take standardized tests. Exceptions are limited to the most cognitively or physically disabled. Subgroup data are disaggregated and reported separately.

- Most large-scale high-stakes tests require the student to select or provide one correct answer or place an answer to the correct position, thus eliminating the possibility of elaboration and explanation.

- Tests are called *developmentally appropriate* but don't consider that all students grow and learn in individual and unique developmental patterns.

- Tests add stress to an already stressful life that comes from food insecurity, neighborhood violence, and other external factors. Stress hormones such as cortisol make it more difficult for students to think deeply and reason rationally. Stress can come from timed tests, material that hasn't yet been taught, or simply the testing atmosphere.

- Interpretation of assessment results. When students learn that they are in the lowest group, they are demoralized, become resistant to learning, and develop a "why bother" attitude.

shutterstock.com/beta757

Restorative Equity

1. If the purpose of tests is to determine a ranking or final score, then multiple measures must be the norm.

2. The consequences of high-stakes testing, such as public reporting of students' scores, need to be stopped to prevent adverse consequences.

3. Alternative assessments that are equivalent to the standards-based traditional measures must be provided. For example, if the standard says to explain the life cycle of a butterfly, give students the choice of responding with words or labeling their drawings.

4. Adapt assessment to students' specific requirements by altering the length of the test, the difficulty of questions, or the complexity of language.

5. Allow learners to show how they construct an understanding of the problem, whether it be mathematical, historical, or literary. One student writes a journal entry of a person crossing the mountains in a covered wagon, another draws a map or diagram of the event, and a third student summarizes a video from Khan Academy.

6. Display and defend how questions align with learning outcomes that were taught. If students are asked to recall, then a fill-in-the-blank may suffice. But if students are being asked to apply, they need to use a parallel strategy to the one taught in class.

7. Include varied levels of complexity and allow choice in responding. Some students may choose one-point questions such as using specified vocabulary in a sentence or labeling an equation. Two-point questions include a Venn diagram comparing two readings about the same topic or writing a mathematical word problem. Three-point questions include changing the main character's decision and then rewriting the ending to the story or writing an equation for a student-designed mathematical word problem.

8. Value and cultivate the requisite social-emotional competencies that support success such as perseverance, self-efficacy, and a growth orientation.

Reflection

1. In what ways is the assessment you are given or design fair and equitable?

2. What changes do you want to make in your assessment practice to ensure fairness and equity?

APPLIED LEARNING

Reflect on a challenge that you are facing. This could be in your classroom, school, or district. Select one of the key ideas in this chapter, such as effectively utilizing the research that informs best practice; planning and implementing assessment that is mutual, reciprocal, and inclusive; or ensuring the technical qualities of assessment: validity, reliability, fairness, and equity.

Use this five-step problem-solving process to develop a plan.

1. What is the problem? Define it in terms of the purposes of assessment and desired outcomes.

2. Brainstorm potential solutions and possible responses. This is a free-flowing nonjudgmental production of ideas.

3. Purposefully evaluate each of the solutions by considering feasibility, personnel, budgets, professional knowledge/skills, and so forth.

4. Select one solution to begin to implement.

5. Design and utilize a strategy for monitoring the process and outcomes. Use this monitoring to continue to regulate and modify the solution.

CHAPTER 2

Restoring Balance

Chapter Goals/Key Ideas

Assessment is a continuous process that informs teaching and learning.

Balance and equity in assessment are the pathways to student success.

Continuously embed assessments to strengthen learning and inform instruction.

Emphasize seamless integration of diverse methods rather than silos of assessment.

Balanced systems unite audience, purpose, and process to meet the needs of all learners.

THE IMPORTANCE OF BALANCE

Assessment is out of balance. Even presidents have acknowledged that assessments must be worthy of our time, of high quality, designed to enhance teaching and learning, and give a well-rounded picture of how students and schools are doing ("Obama Administration," 2015). A balanced approach is a coherent and comprehensive approach. It uses ongoing and embedded assessment while actively depending on growth measures. Multiple methods are valued in order to get a comprehensive and accurate picture of each student's learning. Measures of a spectrum of learning outcomes provide the necessary balance in classrooms, schools, and districts.

Assessment outcomes of students living in low-income settings differ from those in middle- and high-income districts. "These differences reflect that assessments have the potential to reveal social cleavages and the promise to unite diverse communities" (Northwest Evaluation Association [NWEA], 2016, p. 21).

Many of the ideas and strategies throughout this book emphasize assessment that is aligned, relevant, purposeful, clear, embedded, and cyclical, engages learners, challenges thinking, and supports improvement. These ideas form the groundwork of a balanced assessment system that can meet the needs of all learners.

FAMOUS FAILURES

Everyone falters and fails at some point in their life. A popular YouTube video titled "Famous Failures" shows how Michael Jordan, Walt Disney, Oprah, and Steve Jobs failed. The narrator explains that with practice, support, and perseverance, they were ultimately able to succeed. But not everyone succeeds and fails equitably. Other well-known people who overcame failure include Mahatma Gandhi, Nelson Mandela, Lionel Messi, Dr. Seuss, and Jackie Chan.

The data on those who are most likely to fail include those who live in poverty, strive to learn in an unfamiliar language, and face difficulties and disruptions such as inadequate resources, frequent moves, lack of consistent care, family breakdown, neglect of basic needs, and proximate violence. More students worry about failing than actually fail, but a failure mindset reduces a willingness to try and can lead to failure. In these settings, when school data fail to sustain educational policy, the most frequent response is more testing.

Keep in mind that a "test" is nothing more than a strategy. Whether it is selected choice, completion, essay, or a project, it is a way to measure learning; it is only the platform for asking students to show what they know. Additionally, any type of assessment can be used for any purpose. An interactive quiz using Google Forms can be used as a quick informative assessment. An annotated learning tracker completed during a unit of instruction can become part of the summative assessment. Incorporating content vocabulary in a diary or ship's log can show understanding of basic concepts.

Many of the roads in New England meander around corners, across streams, and around bends. When I first moved there, I asked why. I was told that the roads were built on the old cow paths. Rather than straightening the lane, the builder simply paved over the existing cow-way. In assessment, it sometimes pays to meander in order to take in the views and see the hills, valleys, and rivers of learning. Sometimes we have to get off the superhighway of testing to clearly see the villages and the countryside.

Balance in assessment means using varied assessments that measure a spectrum of learning outcomes. From superhighways to meandering paths, evidence of learning can be made visible. While an annual exam provides a snapshot at a particular junction, it is the times where learners slow down and explore more deeply that they develop more meaningful and complex thinking. When assessments are routinely embedded throughout learning, a teacher can tell whether Josef is unable to multiply 12 times 3 or didn't understand the word *dozen* in the sentence and thus can respond more readily.

1. Who is at greatest risk of failure in your school or setting?

2. What are the roots of their difficulties?

3. What assessments do you have in place to overcome and rise above their hurdles?

4. What would you like to change about current practices in order to encourage and support the success of all learners?

5. What's your first step?

TYPES OF ASSESSMENT

To best appreciate assessment, these overarching descriptions of various types of assessments are important to understand.

Summative is administered at the culmination of a period of instruction to display the outcomes of learning. For reporting purposes, it encapsulates and categorizes the performance of a student or group. Decisions made based on summative assessments include promotion, placement, teacher evaluation, and changes to curriculum.

Large-scale summative tests provide information to states, districts, policy makers, and test design services. Given infrequently, they offer a big picture of learning. Classroom summatives are given more often, usually at the end of a unit or marking period. They are used for determining grades on report cards, regrouping, or instructional methodology.

Interim assessments are generally smaller benchmark versions of the large-scale tests. They are used intermittently during the year to assess progress toward readiness for the culminating tests. Each score is recorded and each student monitored to determine ongoing growth. Resources and interventions are provided as needed.

Common assessment usually describes those measures used by a group of teachers in a content area or grade level to ensure that all students were given opportunities to learn, even when teachers used different instructional methods. For example, all the social studies teachers may give the same quiz after the unit on the Revolutionary War to ensure that all students achieved mastery, as one teacher relies on direct instruction, another on technology-based learning, and a third on project-based learning.

Formative assessment includes a spectrum of methods and purposes

(Continued)

(Continued)

implanted into teaching and learning. It is used to monitor students' learning, identify lingering gaps, and guide adjustments to instruction. A teacher may rely on a video with embedded questions using EDpuzzle during class or include frequent check-ins on learning using Traffic Light or graphic organizers. At other times, if there is a sense that learning is not moving forward as planned, the teacher may spontaneously use a nutshelling activity where students explain what they just learned and one way to use the learning. If the teacher discovers that the content is too hard or was previously learned, they can adjust instruction without undue delay. Chapter 3 takes a deeper dive into formative assessment.

SEEKING BALANCE

Balanced assessment is essential for increasing student success and reducing student failure because it provides a holistic view of teaching and learning. A balanced approach provides a comprehensive view of assessment while also illuminating the circumstances and progress of each unique student. Balanced assessment is supported by numerous experts:

- "Large-scale assessment systems that focus on once-a-year summative testing do not provide sufficient information to improve student learning" (Gong, 2010, p. 3).

- "A balanced system of assessments, created both inside and outside the classroom, is needed to support student-centered approaches to learning" (Andrade, Huff, & Brooke, 2012, p. 4).

- David Conley (2014) summarizes this when he says, "Today's resurgent interest in performance tasks, coupled with new attention to the value of metacognitive learning skills, invites progress towards a 'system of assessments,' a comprehensive approach that draws from multiple sources in order to develop a holistic picture of student knowledge and skills in all of the areas that make a real difference for college, career, and life success" (p. 20).

This approach also makes a difference in restoring assessment to its rightful place in education and for ensuring that certain populations of learners are not discouraged by large-scale tests.

PRESSURE POINTS

In one day, in a well-respected educational publication, I read two conflicting reports. One said that states were developing assessments of noncognitive skills and another said that the Department of Education was seeking 95% student participation in standardized content-area testing along with sanctions for those out of compliance. This puts incredible pressure on schools to prepare students for standardized tests while developing and assessing noncognitive proficiencies such as a growth mindset, grit, self-regulation, and interpersonal skills.

Pixabay

The latter (noncognitive) is the foundation for success of the former (academic). As George Farkas (2003) explains, "Poor non-cognitive attribute and skill development may accumulate over time; poor skills and habits developed and internalized early on may lead to less desirable educational outcomes" (p. 542).

It is not an either/or decision. In a balanced system, one supports the other. Belief in one's abilities will support students in doing their best, perseverance will encourage them to work through challenges, and self-regulation will result in learners who can accurately assess their growth as well as identify and overcome obstacles. In practice, this requires lessons that begin with a student's incoming knowledge and beliefs about the topic. It means formative assessment is embedded throughout learning. In addition to developing mastery of content knowledge, assessments must also incorporate noncognitive goal setting and monitoring, metacognitive reflection, and self-assessment. In turn, teachers must be prepared to provide scaffolds, differentiation, and interventions to support a broad range of learners.

Application

Summarize the types of assessment using this anagram. An example is provided to get you started.

The letters can be used anywhere within your sentence.

A

S

Balanced assessment relieS on multiple measures to assess a spectrum of learning.

E

S

S

SEAMLESS AND CONTINUOUS ASSESSMENT

Continuous and *informative* are fundamental principles of all assessment. Yet evidence shows that it doesn't always achieve its full potential. As Lorrie Shepard (2000) points out, "Assessment and instruction are often curiously conceived as separate in both time and purpose" (p. 3). At its core, assessment is intended to be enlightening and instructive. When parents receive grades, teachers receive data, and communities are compared, the opportunity for enlightenment is lost. Too often, only summative statistics are available to the public, who celebrate and take pride or despair, lament, and blame.

To make assessment informative to the student, it must revert to its fundamental principle of providing insights into students' strengths and learning gaps, guiding teachers' responses, and steering students' next steps. When assessment is infused throughout teaching and learning, a continual pulse is taken. In response, students can be encouraged to increase their pace and rhythm, or to slow down and make learning more deliberate. No one learns by simply being told to "skate harder" or "jump softer."

Pixabay

Pixabay

As insights emerge during the course of learning, it becomes feasible to respond promptly in meaningful ways. Teachers can make adjustments to depth, pacing, resources, and grouping. Student motivation is improved when they see that the variance between what they thought they knew and what they really understand isn't all that big. It helps them recognize that closing the gap is achievable, support is available, and scaffolds will be provided.

When Michael Scriven (1967) first distinguished formative from summative assessment, he suggested that formative assessment is most relevant to the developmental stages of programs while they are still malleable. Extending that idea, Benjamin Bloom (1971) describes formative assessment as an ongoing tool for improving teaching and learning. Employing the ideas of Black and Wiliam (1998a), combined with the ideas of many experts, continuous embedded assessment can be summarized as

- provides a clear path of learning, from explicit learning outcomes to visible success criteria;

- integrated throughout teaching and learning, informing learning processes;

- relies on an ongoing and cyclical process; and

- teaching is responsive through adjustments to pacing, depth, resources, and scaffolds.

This restores assessment by shifting students' mindset from what they cannot do to one that emphasizes what they *can* do. It changes the belief that a score is final to one that sees learning as ongoing. It restores a belief in one's ability to succeed and illuminates the path so that students know they can make safe choices, can retrace their steps, and can climb step-by-step on the staircase of success. From the first-grader who says he would make the dog bark louder to the high school student who revises her college essay, ongoing assessment supports learning and raises the quality of student work. It is the cornerstone of growth and improvement.

Formative assessment's proximity to learning, responsiveness to evidence, and relevance to teachers and students set it apart from other types of assessment. According to the Council of Chief State School Officers (Linquanti, 2014),

> continuous formative assessment provides linguistic-minority as well as high-poverty students in particular, with multiple opportunities to develop academic uses of language while collaboratively grappling with subject-matter content and disciplinary practices. (p.3)

Application: Case Study

Mr. Milken has been given a structured lesson plan and learning progression with a fixed schedule for instruction and common assessment. He would like some advice on ways to check-in and respond more regularly on student progress than those included in the lesson plans.

What advice would you give him for why and how to do so?

How can you apply this to one of your own lesson plans?

MERGING TEACHING, LEARNING, AND ASSESSING

While the research is compelling and generally indisputable, assessment that takes place continuously during teaching and learning deserves a deeper dive in relation to restorative practice. Students who are at risk benefit the most from consistent and caring teachers. When these ongoing informative practices are not counted in a final score, dignity and trust are developed. Sound nonjudgmental advice goes much further than negative comments and punitive actions in creating a safe classroom. Deconstruction of goals into actionable learning steps is more effective than measuring solely the outcomes of big-picture standards. It is also important for students to understand that when they veer off the path of learning or do poorly on one test, there will be reasonable, focused, and actionable guidance to help get them back on track. Specific aspects of embedded assessment have been proven to be most effective in a restorative school and classroom. These include the following concepts.

ENGAGEMENT

Unlike teacher-regulated of learning, informative local assessment balances teachers' and students' roles in learning. When Hector says, "I have always failed at math so I stopped trying," Ms. Lomita pulls him back on track with less stressful problems to solve, gradually moving him into higher groups as he demonstrates basic proficiencies and builds confidence. She recognizes that it is not uncommon for students to shut down when facing daunting work. She has days when she feels this way too as new standards, new tests, new technologies, and new school leadership result in too many new challenges all at once.

SELF-EFFICACY

When students believe that they have some level of control over learning, they are more apt to take ownership of their learning. They also develop an intrinsic belief that they are capable of making reasonable decisions about their learning. Mr. Reeza begins his unit by asking students what they know about how policies are legislated by government (C3 Framework, D2.Civ. 13). When he gets blank stares, he asks if they know someone who ever collected unemployment, used food stamps, or had problems registering to vote. When that generates powerful discussion of experiences, Mr. Reeza briefly reviews how policies are written and enacted. Students/small groups then select one policy topic of interest to them, use a structured checklist to learn more about it, and ultimately share with the class on "Policy Day" when a local politician is invited to listen to their soapbox presentations.

MOTIVATION

When students see the outcomes of their educational decisions leading to success, they are more apt to continue to strive for it. This is true for teachers, too. When we see a positive behavior plan making a difference in student behavior, we are more apt to continue to develop our expertise in this promising practice. When students are provided with well-structured opportunities to explore a topic of interest, they are more likely to try alternative strategies. When they can choose the exemplars to demonstrate their emerging skills and knowledge, they are more apt to be motivated. This could be in relation to Mr. Reeza's project on government policy or on any subject where they feel ownership of learning.

SELF-REGULATION

By nature, embedded assessment expects students to consider their progress, accept feedback as a way to improve and guide their next steps. Self-regulation begins with small steps, such as a daily exit slip. For resistant students, their first experience may be a rating scale or a brief statement about what they learned. When they receive feedback acknowledging their synopsis, the next step is to ask how they can use the learning, or for them to write a question about what they have learned. In the classroom, recognize their ideas, share, or publish them as an affirmation of the value of their thinking. Over time, noncognitive skills can be encouraged by reflecting on and annotating their role in learning or explaining how they managed the emotional quality of their response. Ms. Johnson was very pleased when Anika said, "Well, at least I didn't blame you for my bad grade and can explain my disappointment. Now will you help me figure out how to do better?"

SELF-ASSESSMENT

Students can make stronger connections to their learning through routine self-assessment of progress in relation to expectations. As engagement, ownership, and motivation are developed, students also learn to become reflective self-assessors. This starts with a brief checklist that is then annotated and ultimately includes reflections on successes (Wins), failures (Whoops), and resolutions or next steps (Ways). Ms. Jennitas sees growth when Mathias notes his Wins as labeling three 3-D shapes correctly, his Whoops in mixing up 3-sided and 4-sided pyramids, and his Ways of reviewing an instructional video on pyramids.

OWNERSHIP OF LEARNING GOALS AND OUTCOMES

No one likes to be commanded to do something, especially when the demand seems unreasonable or too difficult. Some standards are so large that they are intimidating—for example, "Use words, phrases, and clauses to create cohesion and clarify relationships among claims, reasons, and evidence" (Grade 7, CCSS). For most adults, that would require a lengthy and detailed letter to the editor or a defense of a belief or idea. When goals are deconstructed into achievable portions of learning, the task becomes less daunting. If students are writing about clean water and Adira says the fish are sad because humans have polluted their water, and Ramall states that all households should be given water filtration systems, they each have a viewpoint to defend. When pulled apart, these ideas require a clear statement of purpose, gathering of evidence, organizing and sequencing ideas, and providing support for the position. For some students, this means adjusting the rungs on the learning ladder, possibly by scaffolding the steps. In a nonjudgmental classroom, when students see that each step toward their personal goal is attainable, they are more willing and able to engage with the learning, take ownership, and be motivated to continue.

Table 2.1 illustrates a design of a lesson plan that relies on assessment throughout teaching and learning. It categorizes the instructional purpose of the assessment, suggests strategies, and explains the rationale for using it. It is designed to be flexible for the subject, grade level, teachers' and students' needs.

TABLE 2.1   Fundamentals of an Informative and Engaging Lesson Plan

INFORMATIVE AND ENGAGING LESSON PLAN

Subject/Unit:

Big-Picture Goal/Standard:

Local Objective/Learning Intentions:

Success Criteria:

CONCEPT	STRATEGY	RATIONALE
Attention Grabber	Brain teaser, image, quote, puzzle	Establish a positive tone and anticipatory set
Connections to Prior Learning	Review of prior lesson using a vocabulary matching game	Begin to establish meaning and context for new learning. Foundation for self-efficacy
Preassessment	KWHL, Entrance slips Voting on the best answer 3 Corners: What do you think	Identify entry skills, knowledge, and potential gaps
Initiation	Clarify learning intentions/outcomes New content: Who needs it? Personal story, case study, video	Preview/Spotlight upcoming learning. Capture students' interest and curiosity
Instruction	Delivery of new content and skills by the teacher or another medium Questioning and feedback	Multiple modalities, Engaging, Sequential. Differentiated: Adjust challenge, pacing, resources
Embedded Assessment	Graphic organizers, Nutshelling Quick draw/write, Clear/Unclear, Think-Pair-Share	Engages students, monitors learning, and gathers evidence. Supports peer and self-assessment

CONCEPT	STRATEGY	RATIONALE
Technology for Assessment	Google Classroom/Forms, Socrative, ScreenCast, Kahoot, Plickers, Padlet, Popplet, Quizlet	Increases motivation, student interest, guides modifications
Reflection	Journal, Self-evaluation I used to think ___; now I know ___ Next time I will ___	Personalizes meaning. Illuminates and clarifies lingering misunderstandings

Reflection

Most likely, you would not use all of these informative opportunities during one lesson. What are two concepts and/or strategies that you want to try? Be specific about when and how you would use them.

1.

2.

A wealth of research shows that student learning is enhanced through the use of routinely embedded assessments. "The achievement gains associated with formative assessment have been described as 'among the largest ever reported for educational interventions'. While many teachers incorporate aspects of formative assessment into their teaching, it is much less common to find formative assessment practised systematically" (Organisation for Economic Co-operation and Development, 2005, p. 13).

In turn, teachers need to make sure that the learning progressions are reasonable, learning intentions are clear to students, and criteria for success are evident from the start. Throughout learning, teachers must continually elicit evidence of learning, interpret the evidence, both expected and unexpected, identify short-term and long-term responses, and provide interventions.

Application: Case Study

Ms. Scarlata doesn't understand why her students are so resistant to learning. She works hard to make learning fun, does projects with her students, and tries to engage them in discussion, but all she gets is poor-quality work and brief responses. They don't seem to be able to remember learning from day to day, and seem to just want the right answer to her

(Continued)

questions. She has a district-designed teaching schedule and sequence that she is expected to follow in order to raise test scores schoolwide. With a partner or in a professional learning community, identify the first three steps you would suggest to Ms. Scarlata.

1.

2.

3.

MULTIPLE MEASURES

No one would make important decisions such as choosing a college or changing jobs without gathering information, relying on fact-based resources, and checking with people who have more expertise than they do. Multiple elements of the decision would have to be considered including finances, lifestyle preferences, and future potential. Yet in education, policy and economic decisions are often made based on a small number of indicators using big data, meaning data sets so large they require computer analytics to generate state and district data.

> These data sets, however, often don't spark insight about teaching and learning locally. They are based on analytics and statistics, not on emotions and relationships that drive learning in schools. They also report outputs and outcomes, not the impacts of learning on the lives and minds of learners. (Strauss, 2016, para. 1)

To be fair to all students, a spectrum of measures must be in place. To be useful for all educators, local instructive information is essential.

Voices on Multiple Measures

According to the standards from the Joint Committee on Standards and Education Evaluation (2015), "Strong and continuous learning requires consistent attention to gather, analyze, and effectively use accurate assessment information to guide instruction leading to improved student learning" (p. 4).

The Elementary and Secondary Education Act of 1965, As Amended by the Every Student Succeeds Act—Accountability and State Plans (2016) requires "SEA (State Education Agencies) to have an accountability system that is State-determined and based on multiple measures, including at least one measure of school quality or student success and, at a State's discretion, a measure of student growth" (p. 1).

The National Council on Measurement in Education (1995) states in its Code of Professional Responsibilities in Educational Measurement,

Persons who interpret, use, and communicate assessment results have a professional responsibility to use multiple sources and types of relevant information about persons or programs whenever possible in making educational decisions. (p. 8)

Even with a simple arithmetic problem such as how much is 1 + 1, there are multiple ways for a student to show how he or she reached the answer. Rather than asking students to simply supply the answer, it is more important to provide opportunities for them to explain their answer in order to gain deeper insight into their understanding and misunderstanding.

MULTIPLE MEASURES IN A RESTORATIVE CLASSROOM

On many levels, multiple measures are especially important in a restorative classroom. NWEA (2012) compares zooming in "for a close-up view of the performance of each individual child" to zooming out "by using multiple angles over many moments in time" to explore a full range of achievement (p. 2).

Multiple measures offer multiple opportunities for students to show what they know and can do. In diverse classrooms, decisions are better supported through multiple data points. A single measure gives only a momentary snapshot of learning. Multiple points of evidence support triangulation of data and paint a broad picture of the student.

In schools, teachers make the greatest difference in student learning. "Many factors contribute to a student's academic performance, including individual characteristics and family and neighborhood experiences. But research suggests that, among school-related factors, teachers matter most" (RAND, 2012, p. 1).

To make the greatest difference, especially for at-risk students, proven pathways to assessment are most beneficial. Among these are alignment with learning intentions and success criteria, engagement of students in assessment, and flexibility in assessment. For example, when Atilio is working to master his reading of informational texts, he has a choice of topic and texts, including graphic "texts." He has options in how he represents his learning: producing a video, designing a graphic organizer, comparing source information, or presenting a persuasive speech. These opportunities, in turn, help him develop problem-solving skills and higher-level thinking. This type of ownership encourages follow-through, commitment, self-regulation, and motivation.

Multiple Perspectives: To gather accurate information about learning, assessment must be viewed from multiple perspectives. Each user of assessment has specific needs and purposes. Policy writers, curriculum developers, and program evaluators each look at assessment through their own lens. For example, they may consider whether policy has the desired impact, curriculum aligns with the standardized test, or teacher evaluations are valid.

For teachers, these assessment points are important indicators of learning:

- Student understanding of learning intentions

- Student progress toward success criteria

- Consideration of individual strengths while stretching beyond comfort zone

- Identification of lingering gaps in learning

- Ability to apply learning

- Multiple ways for students to demonstrate achievement of learning outcomes

To support student success, consider these points:

- The value and usefulness of the learning to them

- Their understanding of success criteria and how to achieve them

- Recognition of the progress they are making

- Strategies they can use to support improvement and ongoing learning

- Ways they will be able to demonstrate their mastery

Utilize a spectrum of assessment methods adapted for specific purposes.

1. Traditional methods can be augmented by asking students to explain their answers to selected response questions such as true/false, multiple choice, matching, or fill-in.

2. Constructed response such as short answer and graphic organizer where students can elaborate on their learning.

3. Extended Response: Persuasive essays and analytical writing combined with annotated checklists provide insights into their use of relevant resources, synthesis of information, and production of original ideas.

4. Projects, including performances, presentations, and products, assessed with rubrics that gauge clarity of focus and design as well as deeper learning and complex skills.

5. Noncognitive strategies such as goal setting, progress trackers, and metacognitive reflections that provide opportunities to monitor skills such as prioritizing, self-regulation, and perseverance.

Pixabay

Application

1. To assess a student's understanding of life in another time/place (for example, Mesopotamia), analysis of poetry, or a skill such as learning a new instrument, which two of these strategies would give you more insight/evidence ___ ___, and which two would provide less ___ ___?

   A. A multiple-choice test

   B. A test with completion items

   C. Students creating a "how to guide" on the topic

   D. Students teaching other students what they learned, asking them questions during their presentation

If you said A and B provide less, and C and D provide more, you are ready to move on to the next challenge. If not, refer to the NWEA (2016) publication in the References section for additional insights.

2. Describe multiple measures you would use to assess choices C and D.

Fairness via multiple measures is essential for equity in assessment. Rather than using differences in test scores between groups of learners, rely on differences in learning needs to provide multiple ways for students to learn and demonstrate their learning. John King (as cited in Klein, 2016) cautions that

> the use of these kinds of new indicators has … tremendous potential to advance equity, but that will require the vigilance of parents, educators, and the civil rights community. . . . Otherwise, these new indicators could serve to mask some of the equity and achievement gaps we are working so hard to close. (p. 1)

IN PRACTICE

Mrs. Jackson is explicitly teaching problem-solving skills to her ninth graders. After she teaches and shows examples, her students explore and solve one current educational issue. Her suggestions include healthier school lunches, equity in funding, support for after-school programs, and more/less standardized testing.

Jazari and his group want to improve school lunches. They follow a five-step problem-solving process including identifying the problem, brainstorming solutions, analyzing the ideas, selecting one to act on, and planning a way to measure the outcome. They have choice and options in displaying their learning:

- Prepare a comparative analysis of USDA nutritional guidelines to the lunches that are served.

- Use current research on nutrition to redesign the federal nutrition guidelines. Support your changes.

- Design alternative lunch menus that meet federal nutrition guidelines. Explain your thinking.

- Prepare an informative/persuasive video for the board of education to get them to alter the lunch choices.

- Develop a quiz show titled "Who Would Eat This?" that analyzes the nutrients in foods.

These alternative learning strategies and outcomes could be assessed with

- descriptive rubrics that align with the learning intentions;

- peer review, evaluation, and feedback;

- adherence to a planned learning contract. Contracts can include specific learning outcomes, analysis of the problem, individual responsibilities, selection of substantiated resources, progress log, and evidence of learning outcomes; and

- student-designed "test" questions.

In using multiple methods, Mrs. Jackson can assess content knowledge and analytical ability, and twenty-first century and noncognitive skills such as collaboration, creativity, perseverance, and digital literacy.

Application/Reflection

Consider the assessment strategies you most typically use in your own setting.

Step 1: Select one of your learning intentions.

Step 2: Brainstorm a variety of ways students could demonstrate their knowledge, understanding, and skills.

Step 3: Describe strategies for assessing those learning outcomes.

ASSESSING THROUGH THE TAXONOMY

It doesn't matter whether you rely on Benjamin Bloom's taxonomies, Norman Webb's Depth of Knowledge, learning progressions (Hess, 2008), or other sequences of increasingly complex learning. What matters is that teaching stretches beyond recall and understanding, and learning reaches to higher levels of analysis and production. Even kindergarteners are capable of predicting what would happen in a city where the water levels are continuously rising. I heard one say, "Well, I guess we could swim or paddleboard to school."

MULTIPLE TAXONOMIES

Do you know that in addition to Bloom's well-known cognitive taxonomy, he designed ones for psychomotor (motor mastery, skill development, perceptions) and affective (feelings, attitudes, values, motivation) development? Also consider the amygdala, that small structure in the brain that processes the emotional responses to learning. This is important because whatever the learning intentions, if a student anticipates failure or doesn't like the person who is teaching them, they are less apt to transfer learning to the long-term memory centers. Feelings of exasperation, despair, and loathing will override the circuits of cognitive learning. In addition, social stress such as exclusion and bullying also suppresses learning by stimulating the amygdala to take action on the classic fight or flight response.

There also is no denying the importance of the earliest years in the development of social and emotional skills. Evidence shows that poverty has a negative effect on this part of development, which in turn influences academic outcomes. It is also recognized that "Sustained activation of the stress response system can lead to impairments in learning, memory, and the ability to regulate certain stress responses" (National Scientific Council on the Developing Child, 2015, p. 3). But it doesn't have to be that way.

Most large-scale tests assess cognitive knowledge, primarily at Bloom's knowledge and understanding levels. Even questions identified as "performance tasks," such as these released items, generally require thinking at the lower levels of the taxonomy:

Math: Determine how to make the most use of this gardening plot for the designated vegetables and the space they require.

ELA: Read these four source readings on financial literacy. Which source would most likely be relevant to students? Explain and support your response.

Assessment must be inclusive of the full taxonomy. Once we recognize the importance of using multiple assessment methods and strategies, the next step is to align them with instructional aims. These can be used to develop progressive learning intentions that describe where students are now, what they are aiming for, how we/they will know whether they are moving in the right directions, and how well they achieved. Table 2.2 shows a cognitively based academic sequence followed by questions and actions to prompt higher-order thinking.

TABLE 2.2   Beyond Knowing and Understanding

Math: Counting

Learning Sequence

Randomly states numbers	States counting words sequentially	Accurately keeps track of objects counted	Indicates the last number stated is the total quantity	When objects are rearranged, states the same total number	Continues the sequence when one or more objects are added to the set

Higher/Deeper Thinking

Explain the purpose of the counting you are doing.

What are you trying to count? How could you do that without counting each one individually?

Write questions for a math game the class could play. For example:

Start at 11 and count ten numbers more

Draw a chart showing counting by 2s

Write a story about a mouse (or another animal) trying to count its _____ (you choose)

ELA: Characterization Learning Sequence					
Labels the feeling of a character	Labels one's own basic emotions	Labels complex and higher-order emotions	Explains how an event evokes certain emotions	Explains that the same event can result in individual differences in feelings	Explains how one's emotions can be controlled or modified

Higher/Deeper Thinking

How would the story end differently if the main character exhibited a different emotional response to the other characters and the events? Write a different ending to the story.

Would you act the same way as (name the character)? Explain why or why not.

What question would you want to ask the character or the author?

Create an illustration or video showing the character exhibiting varied character traits.

PLANNING FOR ASSESSMENT

Planning requires a birds-eye view. It means having a specific purpose, uplifting students throughout the taxonomy, and charting interconnected pathways. Too often, higher-level thinking involves moving numbers into the correct sequence, explaining relationships on the periodic table, or motivations of historic figures.

While these are good starting points, if the purpose is stretching beyond knowing and understanding, then students need to become questioners, generate alternative solutions to problems, or interpret images. Here's a three-step process to guide you in navigating restorative assessment.

1 THE FIRST STEP is matching assessment strategy to the learning intentions.

Table 2.3 shows examples of learning outcomes at increasing levels of the taxonomy and strategies for assessing them.

TABLE 2.3 Assessing Levels of the Taxonomy

TAXONOMY LEVEL	ASSESSMENT STRATEGY
Knowing	Associate a name with the different angles labeled A through D in the diagram.
Understanding	Using the list provided, put the sequence of digestion in the correct order in the spaces labeled 1, 2, 3, 4, and 5.
Applying	Conduct a lab experiment on states of water. Record your findings on the data sheet provided.
Analyzing	Explain how culture affects the way an individual views the world and/or the way a person acts in a group. Include examples.
Evaluating	Compare the arguments of people participating in a debate on _____ based on their use of evidence and clarity of statements.
Creating	Write an opinion piece synthesizing multiple views on _____. Draw your own conclusion at the end.

2 THE SECOND STEP is to consider ways to incorporate higher and deeper thinking and noncognitive skills such as dispositions and beliefs about self, learning, and life within more traditional assessments. For example:

- Math: Provide a problem for the class. Don't solve for x, but rather collectively figure out how many wrong ways there are to answer the question. Analyze what's wrong with those answers and then individually calculate the correct answer. Submit your answer with a reflection on the value of learning from mistakes. Exit slip for content learning: Write/solve a problem that demonstrates understanding of how to find the function of x.

- Social Studies: Provide each small group with a problem that a famous figure in history faced. Summarize what that person decided to do. Consider alternative outcomes if that person had chosen another option or life path—for example, John Kennedy and the Cuban Missile Crisis or Thomas Jefferson's purchase of Louisiana. Also consider Martin Luther King Jr., Sir Isaac Newton, Marie

Curie, Rosa Parks, or Harriet Beecher Stowe. Peer review the presentations. Record what you would do if you were in the situations that the famous person faced. Is it the same as their solution? Why or why not?

- Multistep project: Develop a portfolio of learning that includes demonstrations of goal setting, perseverance, and self-regulation. As students review and select their exemplars, they annotate them based on alignment with their writing goals, what they learned from an inferior/lower grade assignment, steps they took to improve their learning, personal traits and habits that contributed to or hindered their learning, and what they learned about planning and designing portfolios.

- Analysis of source material: Each small group chooses a side regarding an issue such as wind power, school uniforms, or privatization of space travel. They use a checklist to validate source material and then debate a team with a diverse view. The debate scoring includes support for position, citation of source material, accuracy and clarity of information, personal contribution, and self-regulation. The debate is rated by a panel of peer judges. Teams reflect on the feedback, describe what they learned, and explain what they would do to strengthen their debate skills in the next round.

- Create a poster or infographic predicting the future of a current trend such as learning from interactive games, genetic engineering, or self-driving cars. Incorporate a metacognitive analysis that includes why they picked the topic, how they learned about it, the best information they found, how they selected the content, and the process in designing their graphic.

3 THE THIRD STEP is to produce a comprehensive map to help students and teachers reflect and analyze students' thinking, affect, and actions. Using concept maps such as Coggle or Popplet, students create, explore, and analyze their thinking, feelings, and actions while they are learning. The box on the side includes a few examples of the properties of each component of the map.

Thinking
Knowledge
Understanding
Analysis

Feelings
Satisfied
Excited
Frustrated
Isolated

Actions
Decide
Collaborate
Design
Revise

Larry Ainsworth (2010) advises teachers to decide what is most important and essential to learn by relying on priority standards.

> Priority standards are a carefully selected subset of the total list of the grade-specific and course-specific standards within each content area that students must know and be able to do by the end of each school year in order to be prepared to enter the next grade level or course. (p. xv)

These standards then help students to make connections to a wider spectrum of learning outcomes. By leveraging the staying power of these durable standards, students build foundations of learning while making connections across disciplines and taxonomies.

IN PRACTICE

In a unit on fables, students analyzed the metaphors, explained their beliefs about the value of learning from fables, and one way that the fable they read influenced their beliefs or behaviors (or alternatively, why it didn't). Armani said, "When I read *The Fox and the Grapes* [Æesop, 2016], I thought the fox was clever, but then realized he really wasn't that smart. Instead of calling them sour he should have found something else to eat because he would have been happier. If I were the fox, I would go home and ask my mom for a snack—maybe grape jelly with peanut butter."

The upper levels of the taxonomy are where students reach higher in their thinking and dig deeper in their learning. In upcoming chapters, we consider how learning progressions and noncognitive strategies build students' capabilities at the upper reaches of learning. This is where we stop to consider the best ways for planning, designing, and using assessments that support higher and deeper thinking.

BALANCED ASSESSMENT SYSTEMS

There are several ways to think about assessment systems. Some view it as a start-to-finish process, somewhat akin to taking a long flight. The students climb aboard, receive instructions at take-off, and are eventually delivered to a destination. Sometimes they get stuck at an unexpected airport or are just plain bewildered and don't know where they are. While it is important to take a birds-eye view of learning, there also must be priorities and strategies to safeguard the arrival at the intended endpoints.

In a balanced system, everyone is included in the planning, implementation, and assessment of learning. A road map and GPS are provided so that the starting and ending points are visible and accurate, and the pathways clear. This system is clear in its purpose, cohesive in its process, responsive to participants, and accountable.

Application

| 1. Select a standard/learning intention from a specific grade/level and content area. |
| 2. Deconstruct into assessable learning outcomes as appropriate. |
| 3. Associate levels of learning through the taxonomy with an assessable outcome. |

Standard/Learning Intention:

TAXONOMY	LEARNING OUTCOME	ASSESSMENT
Knowing		
Understanding		
Applying		
Analyzing		
Evaluating		
Creating		

RESTORATIVE ASSESSMENT

A system may begin with big-picture standards and annual tests. To become operational, it continues through a deconstruction process where the standards become locally assessable. The process also includes interim measures, local methods, and an emphasis on student progress. This coherence assures all learners the opportunity for success. The emphasis becomes growth rather than final test scores.

Consider these three elements in designing your local assessment system:

Audience: Take into account the needs of multiple constituents. Think through the diversity of needs, from policy makers and external monitors to local constituents, students, and families.

Purpose: Rely on the value of a spectrum from large-scale summative to in-the-moment formative. Then disaggregate why, how, and when the measures will be used. Aim for balance in planning for learning and assessment, supporting learning, monitoring outcomes, and guiding decisions.

Process: Appreciate how a cohesive, systematic, and inclusive cycle of assessment can best meet the needs of diverse learners.

Reflection

Questions to consider when reviewing your local assessment system:

1. Who are the users of our assessment system?

   How are we meeting the needs of a spectrum of users, from policy makers to students?

   In what ways is the system fair and equitable for all users?

   How do we inform and respond to assessment feedback and data?

2. What is the purpose of our assessment system?

   What evidence is there that assessments align with our stated purposes?

   How accurately does the breadth of our strategies support our desired learning outcomes?

   How do we show that our assessments are inclusive of the needs of all learners?

3. How well does our content match our purposes and processes?

   What evidence is there that our assessments include all levels of the taxonomy?

   How much attention do we give to noncognitive assessments?

   How effective is our cycle of assessment in supporting student progress? How do we know?

   How thoughtfully are we using our system to support ongoing improvement?

RESTORATIVE SYSTEMS

Somewhere between the extreme ideas of zero tolerance and laissez-faire is a place where assessment finds the balance between accuracy and coherence while still being reasonable and sensible. In restorative assessment, expectations are clear from the start and are supported with clear guidance and meaningful support as students construct and strengthen their pathways to success.

Systemic balance begins when we foster a spectrum of assessments. Policy writers who emphasize large-scale measures must also consider the importance of local assessments. Teachers and students who routinely gather information about learning can merge the daily snapshots into a full compendium.

Only by balancing assessments can we translate big-picture data into local practice. A system of assessment is *not* simply a collection of tests. To be effective, all the parts of a system, from policy to practice, must be comprehensive, interdependent, and responsive. Only then will all students be served equitably.

Insights on Restorative Systems

- Brian Gong (2010) explains that this is needed "because large-scale systems do not provide sufficient information to improve individual student achievement" (p. 3).

- Ted Coladarci (2002) says, "A collection of assessments does not entail a system any more than a pile of bricks constitutes a house" (p. 774).

- Andrade et al. (2012) explain that their "vision of student-centered assessment includes: individualized; focus on growth; engaging; motivating; self-regulation; informative to a variety of audiences" (p. 21).

Balance emphasizes developmentally appropriate learning intentions; valid, reliable, and fair assessments; and use of data to inform and improve teaching and learning.

For most students, academic success is a complex union of content knowledge, skills such as problem solving, and dispositions for learning such as self-regulation and perseverance. Balancing these elements is especially important for students who find success more elusive. Finding the fulcrum between cramming loads of content into short-term memory and embracing the value of strategies for lifelong progress is a challenge that all educators face. For at-risk students, it is necessary to gently tip the scale to the noncognitive side until those habits of mind and disposition required for success, such as mindset, conscientiousness, and interpersonal skills, are achieved. McDonald, Calderone, Bergman, and Boyd (2015) explain that underperforming students are less likely to pursue help. "The skills they need for success can be taught and should be integrated throughout all learning" (p. 12). Because of this, balance is much more important in a restorative setting.

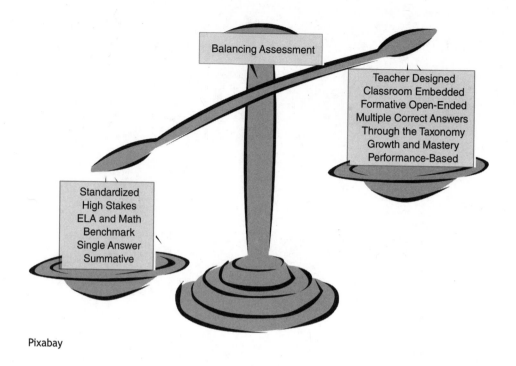

Balancing Assessment

Teacher Designed
Classroom Embedded
Formative Open-Ended
Multiple Correct Answers
Through the Taxonomy
Growth and Mastery
Performance-Based

Standardized
High Stakes
ELA and Math
Benchmark
Single Answer
Summative

Pixabay

Questions for Discussion

1. How can teachers' knowledge and skills in planning, designing, and using multiple assessment strategies guide students' learning and improve instruction? Why is this important?

2. What are the advantages to all students of having multiple ways to show what they know and can do? Think of an example of how this can be used in the classroom.

3. How does the use of best practice in assessment throughout teaching and learning meet the needs of all learners? Consider how this applies to specific types of at-risk learners.

4. What is your vision of a comprehensive and balanced local assessment system? Describe how you would design one that is inclusive, interdependent, and responsive.

5. Using the diagram of balancing assessment, explain how you would increase the balance in your setting/ system. What practices would you like to increase, and what do you want to decrease?

CHAPTER 3

Reinstating Mastery and Growth

Chapter Goals/Key Ideas

Growth and improvement are the cornerstones of mastery.

Mastery is achieved when the sequence and scaffolds enable each learner to succeed.

Well-defined and feasible progressions of learning build the foundation for mastery.

Mastery is through continuously embedded assessments and informative feedback.

Growth and mastery are assessable and reportable.

CORNERSTONES AND KEYSTONES

How would you feel if the first day you played the piano you were expected to perform a concerto with a philharmonic symphony by the end of the day? Would you be more likely to practice extra hard or simply give up and try doing something else with a greater possibility of success? Now put yourself in your students' shoes. How would you feel if you were a ninth grader reading at a third-grade level and were expected to analyze *Romeo and Juliet*? What if you could remember everything on the grocery list your mother told you but couldn't figure out if the one-pound box of cereal at $3.49 was a better value than the buy-one-get-one-free 8 oz. box for $2.99?

In these scenarios lie significant hurdles for at-risk students: In achieving academic mastery, they may start behind and continue to lag behind students with more opportunity. But what if we changed the piano concerto requirement to learning to play a simple version of Beethoven's "Für Elise"? What if you could watch *Romeo and Juliet* performed in plain English or were asked to compare the plot and characters to *West Side Story*? Many would say that those ideas offer a more feasible starting point. So why don't we do this for all students who need extra support in mastering grade-level work? Why are teachers in those settings more apt to be given scripted lesson plans labeled with the required delivery date and time? Even worse, why do we pass students forward to the next grade before they have mastered their foundations, only to face increasing frustration? Restorative assessment means placing the cornerstones and keystones of learning in place before laying on the capstones of large-scale testing.

MASTERY LEARNING

Mastery means that learners have developed and can demonstrate an explicit set of skills and knowledge. Coined by Benjamin Bloom, Learning for Mastery was soon rebranded Mastery Learning (Bloom, 1971). He recognized that while all students can learn, they vary in their rate and depth of learning in the classroom. He also believed that all students can be successful when provided with just-right settings, processes, and resources.

Bloom noted that most teachers deconstructed learning into teachable elements, taught it, and gave students a summative assessment at the end of the unit. He found that when students received support in diagnosing their mistakes, guidance on how to correct them, and opportunities to resolve the errors, their outcomes improved.

Relying on these insights, Bloom sought to combine the best of both direct instruction and individual support by building students' expertise through feedback and response. This formed the foundation of today's practices in assessment *for* learning (aka formative) rather than merely assessment *of* learning (aka summative).

BLOOM'S TAXONOMY

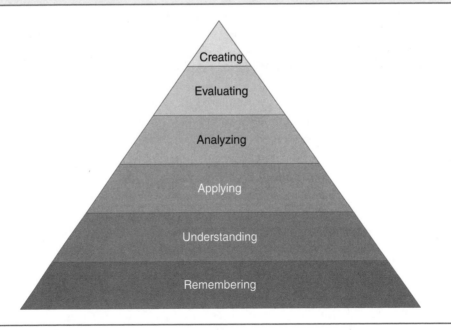

Source: https://www.flickr.com/photos/21847073@N05/5857112597 (CC BY-SA 2.0) Artist: Andrea Hernandez

Over time, mastery morphed into demonstrations of achievement of learning goals through rigorous and uniform testing. When we backtrack to its original intent, it becomes clear that local assessment is at the heart of mastery. With so many ways to learn and so much to learn, it is virtually impossible to teach every student what he or she needs to know in every subject. Knowing what students know and can do in the present and where they are headed next is the first step toward educational success. This is achieved through ongoing formative assessment, defined as: Assessments that align with learning intentions, are embedded throughout teaching and learning, use evidence to provide insight into student understanding, offer feedback that is descriptive and actionable, and inform the teachers' and students' responses. Think about how these processes helped you learn to grow vegetables or swing a bat.

Large-scale tests provide a glimpse of a student's achievement on specific learning outcomes on a given day of the year. But today's learners must be prepared to meet the challenges of the twenty-first century every day. Students must be engaged in meaningful learning at a sequence and pace that is appropriate in relation to their own capabilities. Carol Dweck (2007) explains that the best learning outcomes rely on a growth mindset. This mindset is a direct result of personal mastery. And this personal mastery comes from continuous growth built on feedback and correction that is comprehensible, specific to task and process, guides next steps, and supports self-regulation.

Mastery means more than giving the one right answer on a high-stakes test. Large-scale standards must activate locally measurable outcomes that in turn lead to the assessment of minute-by-minute and day-by-day progress. So how do we go about refocusing on mastery and ensuring the growth of all students?

In Practice

One of the most effective uses of mastery learning I have seen was in an eighth grade prealgebra class. In this mixed group of learners, some were ready for building their algebra skills while others were not. After some experimentation with whole-group teaching, Mr. Cherilla was frustrated. Students who did not understand the new concept and its purpose shut down and at times could be disruptive. He identified a group of students who had mastered the prerequisite skills and positioned one of them in each small group of mixed learners. As the lesson was being taught, the mastery students helped others in their group to understand the concept or support their problem solving. At the end of each segment of teaching, each of the group "guides," as they were called, administered a miniquiz to check for understanding.

Mr. Cherilla took note of whether it was just a few students who did poorly or a larger number. If there were just a few students, he would use the "get-ahead" cumulative activity with most of the class and then help those learners who needed additional support. If there were a larger number of confused learners, he would reteach using an alternative strategy such as an online tutorial while the proficient students worked on a more advanced tutorial.

SUPPORTING AND GAUGING PROGRESS

According to John Hattie (as cited in Masters, n.d.),

> One thing we know from our work in schools is that teachers do not have a shared understanding of progress. When we ask them to identify levels of the curriculum based on evidence of what students can do, the variance in their estimates is frightening. Only by focused discussion and collaboration do teachers begin to understand how curriculum progression works. (para. 10)

Using Hattie's research and insights means taking a step back from the scope and sequence of learning in order to dig deeply into the intended learning outcomes and move them forward in a practicable and student-approachable trajectory.

BLUEPRINTS

Builders use blueprints that show scale, size, and relationships between the features of their designs. Three-dimensional blueprints give additional information about the use of space, entries, utilities, and more. In the classroom, teachers use blueprints that include the standards, instructional strategies, and assessments. They can be hampered by a conventional curriculum that tells them what and how to teach but rarely includes ways to adapt, adjust, and meet the needs of diverse learners.

In general, blueprints illuminate the big picture and inform local learning intentions. They may also recommend or direct instructional practices. Typically, lower levels of the taxonomy are assessed with selected choice and completion questions, while higher and deeper thinking requires more complex and comprehensive measures. In the classroom, this means ensuring alignment between the cognitive complexity of the assessment and the learning intentions. In brief, a typical blueprint is shown in Table 3.1. Following that, Table 3.2 shows a blueprint specific to ELA.

TABLE 3.1 Basic Blueprint for Teaching: From Standard to Assessment

STANDARD	TEACHING METHODS/ LEARNING PROCESSES	DEPTH OF THINKING (TAXONOMY/ DOK)	ASSESSMENT STRATEGY
Content Knowledge: Clarify words in domain-specific texts	Vocabulary building	Knowing	Selected choice
Understanding of Concepts: Use domain-specific words and phrases	Retelling in own words	Understanding	Completion items

STANDARD	TEACHING METHODS/ LEARNING PROCESSES	DEPTH OF THINKING (TAXONOMY/ DOK)	ASSESSMENT STRATEGY
Application of problem-solving strategies	Case studies: Topic related to textual content	Applying	Annotated checklist
Synthesis of ideas into an original presentation	Individual or group-structured project	Synthesis, productivity, creativity	Rubric self and peer

TABLE 3.2   ELA Blueprint from Standard to Assessment

Standard: Use linking words and phrases (e.g., *because, therefore, in order to, for example*) to connect opinion with reasons and evidence.

LEARNING INTENTION	LEVEL	INSTRUCTION	ASSESSMENT
Shows knowledge of linking words when writing	Knowing	Based on curricular and student needs	Completion items on a quiz: Identify the linking words
Uses linking words to connect ideas	Understanding	Based on curricular and student needs	Expository writing assignment requiring at least three examples of linking words
Uses clauses to link ideas within and across categories	Applying	Based on curricular and student needs	Write a fact-based letter to the editor of the local newspaper on (topic of choice). Identify and explain the places and rationale for using linking clauses

Reflection

Here are some questions to consider when designing a blueprint that is effective for all learners:

1. Is the instructional strategy/format accessible to diverse learners?

2. Are the strategies relevant to the depth of learning? Are they flexible for time and content?

3. Is the type of assessment appropriate for all students in the class?

4. Is the scoring based on an objective scoring guide?

5. Is there flexibility in evaluating student responses?

6. Are the questions valid and reliable in relation to the standards, instruction, and student?

(Continued)

7. What's the weight of this assessment in relation to the value of the learning outcomes?

   Think about blueprints you are currently using. Which of these questions are most important to you?

   How will you use them to guide your next steps in planning and improving your progressions?

LEARNING PROGRESSIONS

Progressions turn the sequences of a unit or curriculum into attainable steps. They are the building blocks of success. There are multiple ways to look at these progressions and use them as planning guides that facilitate the alignment of standards with assessment. What is important to keep in mind is that when the sequences for learning are feasible, the learning intentions are clear, and the criteria for success are evident from the start, students are more likely to succeed.

Progressions take the blueprint to deeper levels. Typically, they are displayed as charts or maps showing increasingly complex learning along with multiple ways to assess. They rely on big-picture ideas and large-scale standards that are translated into sequences of successively more complex learning and thinking. An important understanding is that "there is a sequence along which students can move incrementally from novice to more expert performance. Implicit in progression is the notion of continuity and coherence" (Heritage, 2008, p. 3).

Karen Hess (2008) adds to our understanding of progressions by anchoring them to what students already know about the concepts and thinking skills at the start and also considering how they will be expected to use the learning. She also emphasizes that progressions require a "clear and binding thread that articulate the essential/ core concepts and processes" (p. 4). She abides by this example from "Little Red Riding Hood."

1. Remember: Where was Little Red Riding Hood going?

2. Understand: Retell the story in your own words.

3. Analyze: What are some examples of personification in the story?

4. Evaluate: How smart is the wolf? Justify using evidence from the text.

5. Create: Propose your own story in a different place and time that uses a similar plot and characterization to Little Red Riding Hood.

Table 3.3 shows the deconstruction of big-picture standards into more assessable elements of learning.

TABLE 3.3 Deconstructing Standards

STANDARD	KNOWING	UNDERSTANDING	APPLYING	ANALYZING/ EVALUATING
Grade 3 ELA: Describe characters in a story (e.g., their traits, motivations, or feelings) and explain how their actions contribute to the sequence of events	Name the lead character's feelings based on information found in the text	Describe one character's traits based on the actions and feelings described in the text	Explain how a character's actions influenced the sequence of events and the other characters in the story	Expound on how the story or the ending would change if the character showed different feelings or took different actions
High School Geometry: G.CO.12 Make formal geometric constructions with a variety of tools and methods (compass and straightedge, string, reflective devices, paper folding, geometric software, etc.)	Label measurement tools	Explain the different types of tools and methods that can be used in the construction of geometric figures	Apply the definitions, properties, and theorems about line segments, rays, and angles to support geometric constructions using selected tools	Demonstrate the accurate use of a variety of tools and methods (compass and straightedge, string, reflective devices, paper folding, geometric software, etc.)

There is no hard-and-fast rule for making accommodations to this sequence. It can be personalized for learners with varying reading and comprehension proficiencies. Also, the weighting of the responses can be flexible. Ms. Walenca has one group of readers complete steps 1 and 2 individually and step 3 collectively. In another group, she does a quick verbal check of questions 1 and 2 and has students complete question 3 individually, develop a debate for question 4, and has the group work together to complete part 5. When they present their original story to the class, there is a peer-assessment process that measures alignment with the story line, clarity of the character traits, and resolution of the problem.

The example in Table 3.4 illuminates a strategy for engaging reluctant learners by turning them into planners. They write questions about the learning intentions, search for answers, and determine the best way to show what they know about their developing levels of mastery. A pretest can be given to validate their incoming level of mastery. Support is provided during their learning. At the conclusion, students may want to report their learning to an audience of their peers.

TABLE 3.4 Student as Planner

LEARNING INTENTION	QUESTIONS TO ASK	WAY TO SHOW MY LEARNING
1. I have never heard of the idea of natural selection and don't know where it comes from.		
2. I've heard about natural selection and evolution but am not sure about the connection.		
3. I can explain the theory of natural selection and its effects on genetic makeup and survival of species.		
4. Using a diagram, I can track the evolution of a species and identify specific markers of natural selection.		
5. On that diagram, I can predict and illustrate how natural selection will influence the future evolution of the species.		

Based on these learning progressions, students and teachers can develop relevant and developmentally appropriate learning plans. Examples are shown in the following section of increasingly complex progressions. Note that progressions can be written from a student's, teacher's, or peer-review perspective. The numbers in the columns show the number of questions, the type of assessment, and the level of taxonomy for each learning intention.

ASSESSMENT PROGRESSIONS

Assessment progressions extend the ideas of the learning progressions. In addition to showing the sequence of learning, they associate the assessment strategy with learning outcomes at each level of the taxonomy.

Tables 3.5 and 3.6 show examples of learning progressions through the taxonomy with aligned assessments. Note that each intention is matched to a level of the taxonomy and assessment strategy such that all rows and columns are individually subtotaled and collectively tallied to ensure balance.

TABLE 3.5   ELA Assessment Progression

Standard: Use narrative techniques, such as dialogue, pacing, and description, to develop experiences, events, and/or characters.

Focus: Narrative Writing Learning intentions in sequence of complexity	ASSESSMENT STRATEGY				LEVEL OF TAXONOMY						
	Selected Choice	Completion	Perf.	Total	Recall	Understand	Apply	Analyze	Evaluate	Create	Total
1. Students will be able to define and discuss personal narrative in their own words. **Recall**	2			2	2						2
2. Students will be able to recognize narrative techniques such as dialogue, pacing, description, and tone in examples of personal narrative given to them in class. **Understand**	1	2		3		3					3
3. Students will be able to apply narrative techniques such as dialogue, pacing, description, and tone to their personal narrative. **Apply**		1	2	3			2	1			3
4. Students will be able to evaluate the effectiveness of different personal narrative techniques. **Evaluate**	1	1		2				1	1		2
5. Students will use technology to produce a personal narrative. **Create**			1	1						1	1
Total # of Questions	4	4	3	11	2	3	2	2	1	1	11

TABLE 3.6   Science Assessment Progression

Focus: Sound as a Form of Energy: / Learning intentions in sequence of complexity	ASSESSMENT STRATEGY					LEVEL OF TAXONOMY						
	Selected Choice	Short Answer	Extended Resp.	Perf.	Total	Recall	Understand	Apply	Analyze	Evaluate	Create	Total
1. Recognize that vibrating objects produce sound when transferred through another material (air, solid, liquid). **Knowing**		3			3	1	2					3
2. Explain how sound travels through gasses, liquids, and solids differently. **Understand**	1		1		2		2					2
3. Demonstrate how the loudness, pitch, and quality (timbre) of sound can be varied. **Apply**	2		1		3			3				3
4. Describe the properties of materials that reflect or absorb sound through their own investigations. **Analyze**		1		1	2					2		2
5. Design and conduct investigations to determine factors that affect pitch. **Create**		3		1	4				3		1	4
Total # of Questions	3	7	2	2	14	1	4	3	3	2	1	14

Checklist

Progressions of learning can be used in diverse ways depending on grade level, content, and other factors unique to each classroom. Here are some generic questions to consider in designing blueprints, maps, and learning progressions. How will you use them to develop a learning progression for your grade level and content area?

1. ____Does the learning move sequentially from simpler to complex?

2. ____Is the description of the attainment of each level clear to the learners?

3. ____Is the timeframe for the progression feasible for achievement of the learning outcomes?

4. ____Does the teacher have the support and resources to plan and deliver the essential ideas in the progression?

5. ____Are the instructional strategies flexible and supportive of the concepts to be mastered?

6. ____Will students have adequate time and resources to achieve the goals?

7. ____What are the best strategies and resources to move students to the next level?

8. ____Is there flexibility for divergent-thinking, nonlinear learning, and nontraditional learners?

Restorative sequences are highly relevant to struggling, reluctant, and at-risk students. Restorative assessment considers the needs of both the individual student and the class. This means students begin at the most appropriate level of the progression and are supported in their growth toward mastery of higher levels.

1. Begin by preassessing incoming knowledge (or using previous assessments) and then guide students in making connections to prior learning.

2. Be sure students have adequate opportunities to practice new skills before stretching to higher levels. Gently challenge students, with minimal risk and adequate scaffolds, to stretch to the next level of understanding

3. Ensure that students have exemplars and scoring criteria available so they can continuously self-assess their progress toward mastery.

4. As needed, deconstruct the standards and steps into smaller assessable actions, and support the students in setting and monitoring their own goals. Be sure resources are ability appropriate.

5. To avoid frustration and resignation, the level of expectation should match students' current level of understanding.

These elements are important because of variations in incoming knowledge, skills, and dispositions of our students. As Jean Ormrod (2006) explains,

> The cognitive approach to teaching and learning focuses on complex, meaningful questions and problems that make connections with students' life experiences and cultures. Students who are at risk for academic failure

are a diverse group of individuals with a diverse set of needs, and so there is probably no single strategy that can keep all of them in school until graduation. However, a combination of strategies can help many at-risk students succeed and stay in school. (p. 129)

Pixabay

In Practice

Individual Application

What has been your experience with learning progressions? If you have had none, think about a way that you could use them to make mastery visible and achievable. If you have used them, think about ways to improve and strengthen your use of learning progressions as students are supported and guided toward mastery. What else do you need to know and understand before using them successfully?

Group Discussion

There are diverse perspectives on the value of learning progression in the classroom.

In a recent professional learning community conversation, one teacher criticized the idea of individualized progressions. He believed that his own professional evaluation would be compromised if he did not require all students to achieve common standards.

Another teacher disagreed, explaining that if we don't use progression, we will be leaving more children behind. The further upward the standards move, the more difficult it will be for those students who don't have the foundational skills and knowledge to catch-up and move forward.

Where do you stand on this spectrum of beliefs? Elaborate on your thinking. Consider what led you to these beliefs. Are there other ways to look at the situation?

ASSESSING MASTERY

Mastery of content knowledge can be measured through traditional strategies such as selected choice and completion. When learning is based on computations, historical sequences, or literary forms, it is easier to use these conventional strategies to assess student learning. When the learning requires deeper thinking, diverse applications, critical analysis, and synthesis of ideas, the assessments are inherently more complex. When there is no one right answer, learning can be assessed by teachers, students, and peers using rubrics, checklists, and metacognitions. Essential in these methods are

1. clarity of learning intentions and expected learning outcomes;

2. success criteria that are evident and related to the learning intentions;

3. descriptions of the evidence required at varying levels of achievement;

4. alignment of learning outcomes with standards and benchmarks;

5. availability of support and interventions; and

6. opportunities for growth and improvement.

Each teacher, school, and setting must determine and prioritize the knowledge and skills that are most important and most relevant for their students. In elementary grades, where ELA and math are priorities, the prescribed standards are visible, and evidence of mastery comes from preestablished assessments that indicate student achievement levels. Technology such as Socrative, Mastery Connect, Schoology, and other similar e-tools enable the tracking of student growth. But content mastery is not enough to succeed in today's complex world, and traditional assessments are too narrow.

More complex, multilayered, and multidimensional learning needs to be deconstructed into teachable and assessable elements. For example, if demonstrations of creativity and innovation are required, then the assessable elements of imagination and original thinking must be identified and included.

IN PRACTICE

In a unit on world hunger, Mr. Aleva focuses on research skills, analysis of the problem, and synthesis of ideas. But he also wants students, after reviewing a variety of global nutrition programs, to develop one that is unique. They discover Kiva Labs and get excited about the idea of person-to-person assistance and lending. They begin to brainstorm ways to make this work in their own community. In addition to digital literacy, collaboration, and content knowledge, the core elements of creativity that are assessed in this assignment include

- curiosity: an interest in seeking deeper understanding and meaning;

- fluency: production of a number of ideas in response to a need or problem;

- originality: generation of ideas that are new or unusual;

- elaboration: ideas that display extensive detail and complexity;

- flexibility: exploration and consideration of a variety of possibilities; and

- divergent thinking: the ability to combine, modify, adapt, and customize diverse ideas and solutions.

One way for each of the elements to be assessed is with a rubric. An example of three of the elements of curiosity and divergent thinking is shown in Table 3.7.

TABLE 3.7 Assessing Creativity

Reaching the "Proficient" level is required to achieve mastery.

STANDARD	ADVANCED	PROFICIENT	BASIC	BEGINNER	SCORE
Curiosity	I am intrigued by novel elements and new ideas, and actively seek them out.	I am curious about some things and usually willing to explore new ideas.	With help, I can explore and examine new ways of thinking and doing things.	I feel anxious and try to avoid novelty. I am comfortable with the way things are.	
Originality	I can come up with many new ideas on most topics.	I can come up with some new ideas on my own.	If I have some guidelines, I can usually come up with new ideas.	I need help thinking of new things.	
Divergent Thinking	It is easy for me to (1) combine ideas, (2) modify, (3) adapt, and (4) rearrange things to improve outcomes.	I can do two or three of these in order to improve/ change a product or process.	I can use one or two of these strategies, but my ideas are relatively simple and similar to other students.	This is hard for me to do because I tend to see things as they are rather than how they could be.	
Comments					

Another significant element of mastery is metacognition, meaning "being aware of, monitoring, and regulating one's thinking in relation to self, others, learning, and actions" (Greenstein, 2012). Metacognition is an important link between cognitive and noncognitive thinking. Students can be asked to reflect on their thinking in a variety of ways. For example, incorporating metacognitive thinking during project-based learning requires that they annotate the effectiveness of their strategies, analyze obstacles they faced and adjustments they made in response to problems, and identify lingering questions. In a metacognition of their learning,

Mr. Aleva asks his students to respond to these questions as they work on their project:

- What was easiest for you and why?

- What was hardest for you and why?

- How did you decide where to begin?

- How did you know when you reached your goal?

- What would you change next time?

- Explain the difference in your learning between reading about hunger issues and this project where you planned a program to reduce hunger.

Maria says this: "I usually get real bored in class when a teacher talks too much. It makes me start to doodle and then I get into trouble for not paying attention when really I am. I like this project because we could work as a team, picked our own method, place, and time to learn about hunger. I learned so much about what happens to children when they are hungry. It was hard work to show what I learned, how I learned it, and to think hard about the quality of our work, but the rubrics helped. I hope we can really do the program we planned."

At the conclusion of the assignment, students invite guests from local banks and nutrition programs to review their ideas and provide feedback on the design and feasibility of their local Kiva program.

Reflection/Application

Think about an assignment that you have used in the past and consider ways that you can adapt it to include progressive assessment of growth, productivity, and metacognition.

Why are learning progressions and assessment of mastery important for your students and all types of learning?

Assessment as Learning

Maximizing Formative Assessment and Feedback

Formative assessment is a relative newcomer to the vocabulary of education. First coined by Michael Scriven (1967), there is ample research and knowledge about the formative practices that provide the most return on investment of time and resources. These include:

1. Clarity of purpose and outcomes: Students need to know not only why they are going to work hard at building knowledge and skills but also what success will look like. Achievement varies between students, so it is important for them to know how different levels of attainment will be scored. How will they be expected to show mastery of 80% of the new learning? What does it look like when they reach the proficient level of the rubric?

2. Continuous monitoring of progress: When formative assessments are embedded from start to finish, students and teachers can more feasibly measure progress. Preassessments such as a traditional KWHL of poetry or a technology-based graphic organizer on scientific investigations provide an accurate starting point for teaching and learning. During learning, progress can be monitored with a check-in for understanding, such as entering information on an empty outline, analyzing a quote, or completing a "split judgment" graphic that displays key ideas and supporting evidence. For summarizing, students can be asked to change incorrect answers to correct ones on a practice test.

3. In numerous studies, feedback has been ranked as one of the most effective types of formative assessment—but not just any feedback. Telling children that it looks like they worked hard doesn't support progress if their hard work is inaccurate. To be most effective, feedback must be specific to the task and learning objectives, be given in a timely manner, and offer actionable strategies for improvement.

4. Near the top of the list of effective formative strategies are ones that engage learners in planning, monitoring, and self-assessing their own learning. Students self-assess with annotated checklists where they not only rank their research skills but explain how they searched, selected, and validated the resources. John Hattie (2011) suggests that

> this strategy involves the teacher finding out what are the student's expectations and pushing the learner to exceed these expectations. Once a student has performed at a level that is beyond their own expectations, he or she gains confidence in his or her learning ability. (p. 93)

EFFECTIVE FEEDBACK

As with formative assessment, the qualities of effective feedback have been documented. These quotes summarize the essential ideas.

> "Feedback should take place while it is still clearly relevant . . . soon after a task is completed and the student should be given opportunities subsequently to demonstrate learning from the feedback . . ." (Crooks, 1988, p. 439).

> "Feedback to any pupil should be about the particular qualities of his or her work, with advice on what he or she can do to improve, and should avoid comparisons with other pupils" (Black & Wiliam, 1998b, p. 9).

> "Formative assessment includes both feedback and self-monitoring. The goal of many instructional systems is to facilitate the transition from feedback to self-monitoring" (Sadler, 1989, pp. 121-122).

> "The simplest prescription for improving education must be "dollops of feedback"—providing information how and why the child understands and misunderstands, and what directions the student must take to improve" (Hattie, 2009, p. 9).

Although the concepts of feeding up, feeding back, and feeding forward have been discussed by many, Fisher and Frey (2009) offer a thoughtful analysis of the key ideas and description of this multifaceted formative practice in the classroom:

Feeding up means clarifying the goal so that students know where they are headed and why.

Feeding back offers information about learning in relation to achievement of the goal.

Feeding forward helps the student identify their next step.

Application: Compare these examples of feedback. Which one of each pair represents higher-quality feedback and which is less helpful to the student?

COLUMN A	COLUMN B
1. Incorrect strategy. Consider adjusting the x- and y-axes.	Accurate graphing, but remember to label your x- and y-axes.
2. I like the way you engaged the listeners with your questions.	Good presentation skills.
3. It looks like you worked really hard on your poster.	The main ideas are a good start. Use the side panels for the supporting evidence.
4. Let's talk about ways to put the sequence of events in order.	I know you can do better with more effort.
5. Explain your chart in more detail.	Accurate data, but think about alternative conclusions.
Write your own	Ask a peer for feedback

More Helpful: 1.B, 2.A, 3.B, 4.A, 5.B

FORMATIVE ASSESSMENT THAT SUPPORTS MASTERY

There are some things to consider when planning to use formative assessment to support mastery and improvement. Do students and teachers share a common conception of mastery and progress? Do they both know the strategies for achieving mastery?

Mastery learning gives struggling students the opportunity to recognize that success sometimes comes in small steps, but with perseverance and support they can succeed. It is typical for these students to be reluctant to try and fearful of failure. Formative assessment combined with mastery learning enables these students to set their own goals, ones that they perceive as feasible, and then work steadily toward success when the right scaffolds and supports are in place.

Scaffolds, strategies, and interventions to help struggling learners be successful:

1. Ascertain that goals are feasible for the students.

2. Deconstruct complex tasks into actionable portions.

3. Describe each step in the learning process clearly. Include examples. Alternatively, offer a different learning strategy.

4. Assess step-by-step and provide formative feedback on each portion as well as the final outcome.

5. Provide frequent feed-up to guide students in taking their next step.

6. Use an array of assessment methods to empower success. For example, preassessment, formative, and learning logs.

7. Offer authentic applications of learning to all learners.

8. Maintain predictability in the processes of learning and assessing.

9. Assess learning based on the individual student's growth and progress on each step.

> Teachers should continually seek evidence on whether their students are on track to learning what they need to if they are to reach the goals. Also look for indicators of problems they may be having. And then for responding to that evidence get them back on track or alternatively, adjusting the track. This, of course, is a description of formative assessment in action. (Corcoran, Mosher, & Rogat, 2009, p. 8)

When using these practices in a restorative classroom, in place of a lack of effort, avoidance of work, and adversarial behavior, students can see the purpose and value of learning. They take ownership of learning and assess personal progress. Several positive outcomes emerge from this, including increased effort, attention to task, perseverance, and pride in success.

Mr. Havelson explained that he tried every ploy he knew, from writing out explicit directions to rewards and consequences, to no avail. "So I began with structured and sequenced preassessments that aligned with my instructional aims. Students were then able to sequence their learning based on their achievement on the preassessment. Each student had a learning tracker so they could see their progress. This positive experience changed mindsets and behavior."

Mrs. Jaida said, "I gave up on normal distributions and let students track their own growth curves. What a wonderful math learning experience that turned out to be!"

Ms. Neela explained that "it was a lot of work to get started, what with deconstructing tasks, sequenced learning plans and varied assessments, but my students' scores soared. They became enthusiastic and engaged learners."

Reflection/Application

Yogi Berra said, "If you don't know where you are going, you will end up somewhere else."

In relation to formative assessment and mastery learning:

1. What are the best ways to engage students as they grow toward mastery?

2. Why and how are you currently using formative assessment and mastery learning? If you are not yet, where do you want to begin?

3. How do you respond to and report the information and data about student progress?

4. How can you convince educators and families that this is a valid practice?

Reporting Growth

"Although the metaphor of growth is conceptually appealing, finding a way to characterize growth numerically in a manner that leads to valid and reliable inferences is extremely challenging" (Briggs et al., 2015, p. 1).

GROWTH MEASURES

Inherent in the attainment of mastery is growth. The word *maestro* originates from the same Latin root. To become a maestro requires progressive proficiency in reading music and playing instruments, but more important, synthesizing the entire orchestra into a cohesive unit. Mastery takes time and practice to become proficient. Relying on growth measures requires a foundation of

1. clear learning aims and outcomes,

2. disclosure of the strategies that will be used to assess learning,

3. criteria for achieving each level of achievement of the learning outcomes,

4. comprehensive descriptors of the performances and exemplars expected/ required,

5. determination of the level of achievement required to progress to the next standard or learning outcome,

6. alignment between scoring rubrics and grading system, and

7. interventions for students who are not yet achieving mastery.

These practices are relevant to all students, whether they are on free and reduced lunch or have language, cultural, and cognitive variations. All students bring varying beliefs, expectations, and backgrounds to learning. Assessing growth means starting with the foundations the student brings and then supporting and constructing further learning. As David Ausubel (1968) says, "The most important single factor influencing learning is what the learner already knows. Ascertain this and teach him accordingly" (p. vi).

If equity and fairness in grading are the goals, then the focus must be on progress from the beginning of learning to the point of assessment. While traditional grading is concerned with numbers, especially final scores, standards-based grading is focused on the growth of learning. Shirley Clarke (2001) explains that students "are more motivated and task oriented if they know the learning intention of the task, and also better able to make decisions about how to go about the task" (p. 42). Also, they are better able to focus on the purpose of the learning rather than the activity, stay on task, and take responsibility for learning. In the end, this leads to student self-assessment based on clear learning aims and success criteria.

There are examples of blueprints and progressions earlier in the chapter. Table 3.8 shows an assessment progression explaining how growth can be characterized numerically. It incorporates the essential ideas of quality assessment; in addition, each of the scoring criteria can be weighted to reflect their relative importance, significance to learning, benefits, or utility. This is based on these principles:

1. Standards provide a common foundation of big-picture aims for all learners.

2. Deconstruct standards so they are teachable and relevant to each learner.

3. Learning intentions and success criteria represent increasingly complex progressions of learning, from basic vocabulary to the synthesis of ideas into original outcomes.

4. Assessment includes a spectrum of strategies, from selected choice to projects and performances. These provide opportunities to demonstrate increasingly complex learning in varied ways.

5. Performances and evidence of learning can be designed to be flexible in order to enable all students to display emerging abilities.

6. These assessable and tangible learning outcomes can be aligned and merged with the requirements of most reporting systems.

TABLE 3.8 Assessment Progression

Standard: NGSS ESS2.C Water cycles among land, ocean, and atmosphere are propelled by sunlight and gravity. Density variations of sea water drive interconnected ocean current. Water movement causes weathering and erosion, changing landscape features.

	MAESTRO	MASTER	INTERN	ROOKIE
1. Learning Outcomes/ Success Criteria	Plans and carries out an investigation using multiple variables and provides support for solutions	Follows a planned investigation of influences on weather patterns	Demonstrates understanding of the water cycle when presented with a model	Recognizes the vocabulary of water cycles
2. Strategies	Plans and follows the scientific methods, gathers data, and presents analysis of data	Accurately follows the plan, predicts outcomes, compares results to prediction, and accounts for differences	Labels and explains the effect of wind, landforms, and oceans on a visual model of the water cycle	Fills in blanks in a narrative on water cycles using vocabulary from a word bank
3. Evidences	Self and peer assessment of strategy, data, and analysis based on a rubric	Annotated checklist of steps in the investigation	Labels and explains the determinants of local weather patterns	Fills in the blanks with 70% accuracy

(Continued)

TABLE 3.8 (Continued)

	MAESTRO	MASTER	INTERN	ROOKIE
Attainment Level Score Conversion	Exemplary 90-100	Proficient 80-89	Developing 70-79	Emerging Below 70 with annotation

√ Check off the Scaffolds, Supports, and Modifications Provided	__Deconstruction of standard
	__Adjustment to number and complexity of vocabulary required
	__Use of feedback for improvement
	__Completion of missing elements that provide additional evidence and/or raise quality of work submitted
	__Teacher or peer support_____

CALCULATING GROWTH RATES

Ms. Bonano was tired of being labeled a low-performing teacher. So one year, in collaboration with other content-area teachers, they embarked on a year-long experiment. They all gave the same preassessment that was designed to be a mini-version of the final exam. Her class met at the end of the day, when no aides or support were available, and as she would say, with no disrespect intended, "It seemed like their meds had worn off." More likely it was their patience, self-regulation, and perseverance that were fading. She shifted her instructional strategies and tried some restorative assessment strategies. At the end of the year, her class still had the lowest scores. But when she calculated her growth rates, it was astounding. They achieved greater growth than the other classes. She went into the principal's office and with a big smile on her face, explained that she was no longer a low-performing teacher.

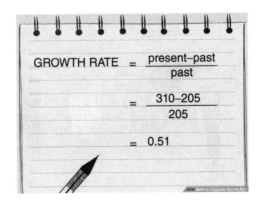

$$\text{GROWTH RATE} = \frac{\text{present} - \text{past}}{\text{past}}$$

$$= \frac{310 - 205}{205}$$

$$= 0.51$$

CHANGING ASSESSMENT MINDSETS

The assessment mindset of lower-performing students can include anxiety, avoidance, and passive refusal. Students might simply put their heads down on their desk or doodle on their test paper rather than risk another failure. Consider how these few changes can make a difference in students' thinking about assessment.

- From prescriptive methods to research-based best practices

- From fixed to adaptable assessment strategies

- From summative outcomes to formative skill-building

- From external mandates to student-engaged learning goals

- From organizational accountability to student accountability

- From superficial knowledge to higher and deeper thinking

Think Like Yogi Berra: "It's not over till it's over." So it goes with assessment. After we assess student learning outcomes, decisions need to be made about how many are expected to show mastery, at what level, and what to do about those who don't. It is not realistic to expect every student to earn a perfect score, but it is realistic for the majority to achieve a predetermined set point in relation to the learning intentions. Then, make decisions about what to reteach, how to reteach, and how to enrich for those who achieved.

Teach Like Yoda: "You will only find what you bring." Yoda is a patient tutor and also a no-nonsense teacher. By perching on Luke's shoulder, he develops an understanding of the problem from Luke's view and creates a personalized learning path that is built on step-by-step progress toward mastery of the Jedi way. Be sure to embed formative assessments throughout your teaching and learning to monitor students' fulfillment of their learning goals. "Do or do not. There is no try."

Assessment, by design, is mastery-based rather than time-bound. This doesn't mean there are endless opportunities to retest but rather that a balanced and comprehensive approach to assessment can benefit all learners. When multiple methods, including a spectrum of strategies from in-the-moment classroom assessment to large-scale national and international measures, are routinely used, then all students have opportunities to show improvement and demonstrate success. In a comprehensive, responsive, and restorative system, assessment is informative in multiple ways: immediately in the classroom, locally at the school and district level, as well as later on for state and national policy makers.

Reflection

1. Reflect on three ideas from this chapter that you want to use.

2. Consider why they are important to you, your setting, your students.

3. What outcomes do you anticipate from using them?

Application

1. How will you convince others that mastery is the true intent of assessment?

2. Try explaining mastery learning to a Martian. What questions would "it" have?

3. Beyond learning content for standardized tests, what elements of mastery are most important to you, your team, your school. Establish two to three priorities to work toward. For example:

We want to develop blueprints to help us deconstruct standards into teachable and assessable nuggets.

We want to convince others that growth is more important than final test scores, especially for at-risk learners. We want to propose that idea with clarity, purpose, and process.

CHAPTER 4

Refocusing on Learners

Chapter Goals/Key Ideas

Developing assessment-capable learners must be a purposeful priority.

Students' self-assessment is built on proficiency in monitoring and modifying learning.

Learner-focused assessment is engaging and personal.

Restorative assessment emphasizes growth and improvement that sustains all learners.

STUDENTS AT THE CENTER

Pixabay

Education was intended to be about our students, their learning, and their future. Today it seems to have shifted to policy, economics, and politics. It will take a collective effort to move the scale back to center: to equalize the needs of learners with the requirements of the larger system. Students are not demographics but rather individuals who are educationally interdependent on many levels: family, peers, community, country, schools, and classroom. In relation to assessment, this means starting from the inside—the student—and working outward to put together a system that works for each student.

When schools begin to falter, it is not uncommon for external forces to seek control. National, state, local, for-profit, and nonprofit groups step in to guide the school or district in revising curriculum, adopting new resources, selecting additional benchmark tests, and evaluating teachers' performance. In many places, the underlying problems are not addressed and the remedy is temporary or superficial. Too often, students are left out of these conversations.

Reversing this means starting with the students. Putting students at the center means assessing learners rather than measuring teachers and communities. Relying on the theory and research on what works best for students, applying insights from the cognitive sciences, and considering noncognitive foundations of learning provide a solid foundation for supporting mastery, growth, and individual success. This is especially relevant to vulnerable learners who may not have the necessary foundational knowledge, self-regulation, or resiliency skills.

> Student-centered assessment embodies sound assessment practices that can be incorporated into any educational setting but are especially critical in student-centered learning contexts, where active engagement in learning and responsibility for the management of learning are core assumptions. (Lea, Stephenson, & Troy, 2003, p. 321)

In practice, Ruth may need to develop a bulleted list using movable sticky notes to arrange her ideas about animal habitats, while Safar does better with a graphic organizer that gives him flexibility in extending his thinking about the meaning of communities. In this way, they both have personalized ways to demonstrate mastery of coherent content.

ASSESSMENT-CAPABLE LEARNERS

Assessment-capable learners know where they are heading, have the resources to get there, and continuously monitor their progress. "They are able to evaluate the worth of their performance and identify their strengths and weaknesses with a view to improving one's learning outcomes" (Klenowski, 1995, p. 146).

Students who are able to regulate and assess their own learning rely on these abilities and strategies.

1. Understand the learning intentions and success criteria.

2. Set goals and track progress in relation to the purpose and outcomes.

3. Analyze work for evidence of learning.

4. Recognize gaps and choose/use strategies to improve their work.

A classic analogy is that the assessment-capable chef checks the ingredients before beginning and continues to monitor the flavor, aroma, texture, appearance, and doneness during cooking. Compare this to the less tuned-in chef who simply chops, mixes, heats, and serves.

CLEAR AND VISIBLE LEARNING INTENTIONS

When students grasp the learning intentions, they can express what they know, ask questions about points of confusion, and recognize what they don't yet know. When students have seen examples of products at multiple levels of achievement, they have a deeper understanding of what is expected. When there is systemic alignment, students can see where they are headed and how to get there.

For students to understand the learning intention, they must also understand its vocabulary. For example, a grade four math standard says, "Multiply or divide to solve word problems involving multiplicative comparisons." For many students, saying "Solve problems using multiplication and division" would be easier to understand.

Before and during learning, a teacher can make the learning intentions more accessible by deconstructing them. After learning, the students share their own examples as part of their concluding collaborative assessment. In their own words, students keep track of their "I was able to" "And now I know" statements by putting the learning outcomes into their own words.

A sixth-grade ELA standard says, "Compare and contrast the experience of reading a story, drama, or poem to listening to or viewing an audio, video, or live version of the text, including contrasting what they 'see' and 'hear' when reading the text to what they perceive when they listen or watch." In his own words, Marcus says, "I will compare the traits of characters in the Harry Potter book to the same characters in the movie version." He uses a graphic organizer that compares the characters' appearance, behavior, and motives. Table 4.1 shows an abbreviated version, as Marcus's version included scene illustrations and descriptions.

Marcus gets feedback from peers and his teacher on his accuracy, evidence, and detail. When he is not satisfied with his impending score, he uses what he has learned about goal setting and self-assessment to guide revisions. His teacher also gains insight on the importance of deconstructing and unpacking the learning outcomes from the start. She decides that next time she will begin by talking about students' experiences and engage students in a sensory activity where they first can only see a band play, then only hear their music, and then compare their experiences using a Venn diagram.

TABLE 4.1 Book-Movie Character Comparison

CHARACTER	BOOK	MOVIE	BOTH
Harry	Disheveled hair More assertive: Took control of Quidditch, told people what to do	Straight, combed hair Less assertive: Couldn't take control of Quidditch game	Empathetic Analytical
Ron	Freckles Reliable, life of the party	No freckles Bumbling; a dud as a friend	Understands magic
Hermione	Somewhat attractive More condescending	More attractive More compassionate	Nerdy, brave, smart

Application

Analyze the alignment of each of the three assessments with the learning intention.

Learning Intention: Determine the meaning of words and phrases in a text

Assessments:

1. Using the context of the story, explain the meaning of "loud *racket*" and "a *plot* to raise vegetables." What else could these words mean in a different context?

2. Write a poem about what you have read using words from the reading.

Underline and define the words as you use them.

3. Give an example of a simile, metaphor, or idiom. Pick one and explain why, when, and how you would use it.

Analysis: Most teachers select number 1 because the students are required to understand the words within a specific text and also extend that understanding to explain different meanings of the same word. Number 2 does not identify the intended vocabulary. Number 3 diverges from the intent of the standard.

STUDENTS AS GOAL SETTERS

Once students have deconstructed the standards and identified their own learning aims, they can translate those aims into assessable goals and learning outcomes.

"Student-centered assessment involves the active engagement of students in setting goals for their learning and growth, monitoring their progress toward those goals, and determining how to address any gaps" (Andrade, Huff, & Brooke, 2012, p. 2).

Marcia wants to get higher quiz scores in the next quarter, but she finds it difficult to develop a plan she can follow. When she learns that the best goals are SMART (Specific, Measurable, Achievable, Realistic, and Time-Bound), she begins to see how to deconstruct her goal into feasible steps. With help from Mr. Webster, she shapes these goals:

1. I will record my learning during class and, as needed, check with my teacher to make sure it is accurate.

2. When I am confused, I will ask for clarification from the teacher or peer leader.

3. I will use my notes to prepare for assessments by organizing, reviewing, and aligning them to the teacher's study guide.

4. If my scores do not improve, I will meet with my teacher to talk about alternative strategies for success. Last year, I was able to explain my answers to multiple-choice questions so my teachers could see what I know and didn't know, and I could earn partial credit. Maybe we could do that again this year.

When students are goal setters, they understand the diagnostic, formative, and summative strategies that will be used. When they monitor their learning, they can readily note progress as well as areas for continued growth. In turn, engagement and motivation increase.

STUDENTS AS SELF-ASSESSORS

Research reveals that students are very good at predicting their achievement level. It also shows that "self-assessment contributes to higher student achievement" (Ross, 2006, p. 1). Self-reported grades are at the top of John Hattie's (2011) visible learning strategies. He explains that the teacher's job is to move students past adequacy by teaching them the skills needed to exceed their expectations.

> The aim is to get the students actively involved in seeking this evidence: their role is not simply to do tasks as decided by teachers, but to actively manage and understand their learning gains. (p. 88)

Goals are the external messages about learning expectations. They are translated by students into actions and behaviors. If we expect students to raise their expectations and assess their own learning, they must have the necessary supports to reach those intentions. At the same time that there is optimism about students as assessors, research illuminates the pathways to ensure they thrive and succeed in that role.

Five steps in developing self-assessment skills: Students will

1. recognize the importance of alignment between learning outcomes and learning actions,

2. set clear expectation for their learning outcomes and performance,

3. define challenging yet achievable goals,

4. identify and plan the strategies and steps to success,

5. predict the outcomes specific to each learning target,

6. continually monitor and self-assess progress, and

7. reflect on learning outcomes and recognize strategies for improvement.

When students set feasible and achievable learning outcomes and have the support, confidence, and skills to achieve them, they become the best assessors of their own learning. All of these ideas affirm the value of self-assessment in the classroom.

In Practice

Armando is struggling with the vocabulary in a new unit. He and the teacher develop a three-week plan that aligns with its intentions, sequence, content, and design. In the first week, he records and defines the new vocabulary. In the second week, he searches for ways this vocabulary is used in the assigned readings. In the third week, he incorporates the vocabulary into his summary of learning. Each week, he tracks his progress with a simple graphic organizer as shown in Table 4.2

TABLE 4.2 Cyclical Self-Assessment

MY GOAL	MY ACTIONS	MY OUTCOMES	MY NEXT STEPS
1. Learn five new vocabulary words.	Record and define the words.	I spelled four right and defined three correctly.	Correct the mistakes I made. Use those words in Step 2.
2. Find the vocabulary words in my readings. Describe how they are used.	Choose readings of my interest at my reading level.	Hmm, I noticed that *object* can have multiple meanings but was used as a verb.	I found four of the words and will ask my teacher to help me find more readings.
3. Use and define the vocabulary words when I summarize my learning.	I will use the words in an illustrated story about alien worlds.	i.e., remote, eerie, orbit	I spelled them all correctly but need to review the definitions of two.

Image Source: Pixabay

STUDENTS AS ADJUSTERS, AMENDERS, AND UPSKILLERS

Upskilling is one of my new favorite words. It implies that the foundations of learning are already in place. It means starting with what the learner knows and can do and then improving upon it. This is true when learning to cook as well as learning how to "Apply concepts of density based on area and volume in modeling situations" (CCSS HSG.MG.A.3), or writing a persuasive essay using evidence and reasoning.

Students that know the progression of a standard or learning intention can ascertain where they are in the process, make adjustments, and move learning forward. This insight can come from their own review of their work, peer feedback, observation of others' performance, or assistance from a teacher.

When the previous steps of clear targets, personalized goal setting, and self-assessment skills are in place, students begin to own their role and take responsibility for improving their learning outcomes. Two key studies, one by Fernandes and Fontana (1996) and another by Brookhart, Andolina, Zuza, and Furman (2004), show that students who were taught strategies for routinely engaging in self-assessment had higher levels of success than those who were not exposed to the strategies. These students were less likely to attribute success to external factors and more apt to recognize that it came from study skills, effort, and deeper engagement in learning.

In Practice

Mr. Alak uses the self-assessment shown in Tables 4.3 and 4.4 to help students own the process and outcomes of their learning.

TABLE 4.3   Step 1 Student's Self-Assessment of Incoming Knowledge and Skills

What do I know now about this topic, idea, or question?	
What do I think I will learn from this lesson/unit? In my own words, the goals of learning are_____	
In addition, I am curious about and want to learn_____	
Why do I need to know this? How will I use it?	
How will I be involved in my learning: What is my role, steps, and tasks? What strategies will I use?	
What kinds of support can I use to help me learn, ask questions, find good resources, etc.?	

(Continued)

TABLE 4.3 (Continued)

How can I get informative feedback to guide and monitor my growth?	
How will I know when I am successful? What will it look like?	
What do each of these mean to me as I start my learning: Learning intention 1 Learning intention 2 Learning intention 3	

He later asks students to explain the learning intentions in their own words, describe what they have learned about each intention, how they learned it, and can now confirm with evidence what they learned.

TABLE 4.4 Step 2 Student Self-Assessment of Process and Outcomes of Learning

In relation to learning intention 1 and the success criteria, I now know and can do_____.	
In relation to learning intention 2 and the success criteria, I now know and can do_____.	
In relation to learning intention 3 and the success criteria, I now know and can do_____.	
When I compare my work to the goals and success criteria, I become aware that I still am learning or wondering_____.	
I am now working at this level of the scoring scale _____ because of this evidence.	
Here's what I did to achieve this level _____.	
I still need help with_____. I can get this help from _____.	
I have these lingering questions: _____.	
This is what I want to commend about my learning _____.	
This is what I recommend to improve my learning _____.	
Here are some ways I can use my learning _____.	

All students can be users of data. Even the youngest learners can monitor the number of vocabulary words they can spell before and after a unit on weather. Older students can analyze their quiz score to discover whether it was the vocabulary or their ability to synthesize the concepts of atomic structure.

Assessment was never intended to be kept secret. Students need to be in the know about their own learning, its purpose, and their progress. This is especially true for students who face greater challenges in learning. Sometimes it is hard for students to understand why they were not as successful as they expected. You may hear Appolo say, "I studied really hard" or "I tried to do my best." That may lead to a conversation about what they need to learn, how to best study it, and the ways they will be expected to demonstrate their learning. Throughout learning, it is essential to emphasize growth and improvement. Data must be demystified, clarified, and translated to plain language. In this way, everyone gets the support they need in doing the hard work it takes to accomplish their personal best.

Reflection on Assessment-Capable Learners

Use this scale as you plan to upskill your proficiencies and knowledge of assessment-capable learners. Rate yourself from 1 to 4, with 1 being "lots of room for improvement" to 4 being "students are highly skilled"

1. _____Learning intentions are visible and clear to students from the start.

2. _____Students can explain in their own words the expected outcomes before they begin.

3. _____Students are able to determine where they are at the start of learning.

4. _____Students have opportunities to personalize their learning goals.

5. _____Students track their own progress during learning.

6. _____Students receive feedback from self-reflection, peer review, and teachers.

7. _____Students use feedback to improve the quality of their work.

8. _____Students ask and answer questions that relate to their learning processes and outcomes.

9. _____Students can clearly describe their evidence of learning.

10. _____Students can accurately plan their next steps in learning.

11. _____At the conclusion of a segment of learning, students can reflect on their planning, actions, and outcomes with precision and depth.

(Continued)

Application

1. Consider the amount and the types of ways you currently support students as self-assessors.

2. Whether you want to build assessment-capable learners or want to more deeply empower students in that role, name three steps you will take in that direction. For example:

I will use a graphic organizer to explain what they thought they were going to learn in comparison to what they actually learned in this lesson/unit.

I/we will . . .

I/we will . . .

I/we will . . .

Even after all this, as Forrest Gump said, "You never know what you're gonna get." In one class, Ramona responded with, "I thought I was going to memorize the formula for determining the area of a rectangle. But now I am really excited to show my parents how I figured out how many square yards of orange shag carpet I need for my room."

PERSONALIZING ASSESSMENT

In the real world, there is not much where one size fits all. From T-shirts and bicycles to Lexile and font size, most of what we do and use requires some degree of personalization. When learning is personalized, students have opportunities to learn at their own pace through the learning channels that are most relevant to them. Although we live in a world of personalization and choice, this doesn't mean that every student gets a customized robotic tutor seated next to him or her. Rather, it means that learning pathways are flexible, resources are variable, and pacing is adaptable.

As we move away from the factory model of education, we gain greater flexibility. Personalizing learning provides opportunities for authentic learning experiences while emphasizing progress toward mastery. In these classrooms, learning and assessing are interconnected.

Somewhere in between the advocates for differentiation and the voices for extreme personalization through emerging technology lie the best ideas for personalizing assessment, where students set their own goals, monitor their progress, and provide evidence of learning in diverse ways. This is both a necessary and feasible approach in today's diverse classrooms.

Rather than relying on standardized test scores that measure a narrow spectrum of knowledge and skills, personalized assessments reveal learning from multiple perspectives. This includes constructed response questions, portfolios, projects, performances, and products of learning that are assessed using gauges such as validated scoring guides where a student's performance aligns with explicit learning outcomes.

For example, if students are expected to "use frequently occurring conjunctions" (CCSS L.1.1.G), they might be able to show their understanding through this multiple-choice question: Fill in the blank with the correct conjunction. I like chocolate ___ not vanilla. Select from these word choices: or, if, but.

However, most educators would agree that moving the word into the correct box on a computer screen is not a performance task but rather another version of selected choice. Alternatively, children could write a story (of their pick of genre or topic) using the conjunctions *and, so,* and *but*. In this way, students select the theme, write about it using their choice of fiction or nonfiction, and receive constructive feedback that they use to improve their work.

Progressing Toward Personalization

1. Standards are deconstructed into achievable and measurable portions also known as learning intentions.

2. Achievement markers and success criteria are evident.

3. Pathways and processes for reaching the goals are flexible.

4. Students and teachers work together to identify baseline knowledge and skills.

5. Students, with teachers' support, formulate relevant and realistic learning goals.

6. Progress toward well-defined learning outcomes is continually monitored.

7. Flexibility in learning strategies/modalities and assessment methodology is evident.

8. Multiple pathways and methods for students to demonstrate their learning are clearly defined.

9. Formative assessment and actionable feedback are embedded throughout teaching and learning.

10. Lingering gaps are addressed prior to any summative measures.

LOCAL, SMALL-SCALE, INFORMATIVE SETTINGS

By honoring our students' needs, strengths, and proclivities, the focus of assessment remains on the learner. The essential question is less about what the learner needs to know and do, and more about what change in the learner's knowledge and skill are anticipated and desired. When a student answers a question about the qualities of heavy metals by explaining the music of Metallica (true story), it's time to clarify and refocus learning. Ms. Mashala briefly explains the Latin root of *metal* and sends the students on a search of examples of heavy metals such as arsenic, lead, and mercury. To engage students, she also asks how that informs the genre's name. Locally, it is more feasible to delve into the meaning or process of learning in ways that standardized tests cannot.

Local assessment systems place students at the center. This starts with big-picture policy that is translated into locally actionable practice. One district wanted to develop a looping routine in which each step, from standardized tests to minute-by-minute formative assessments, incorporated a functional response at the local level. In this way, the primary purpose becomes diagnosis and response rather than scoring and reporting.

For some students, this means progressive assessments that identify the students' starting point as well as the requisite skills and knowledge to progress to the next level. Throughout this process, learning is recorded, feedback is provided, and improvement documented by aligning learning through sequential levels.

Emerging

The students can reproduce the learning as it was originally presented to them.

Developing

Able to see similarities between what was originally presented and ways they can use that in an alternative situation, make inferences, or draw conclusions.

Exemplary

The students are able to select and utilize specific knowledge and skills in a unique situation/setting for a purposeful conclusion or outcome.

John Hattie (n.d.) explains that "Visible learning and teaching occurs when teachers see learning through the eyes of students and when teachers help students become their own teachers" (p. 1). This happens best in local settings where local teachers know their local students. It is especially important in restorative assessment, where students may struggle with grade-level standards and need additional supports to achieve their goals.

INVITING AND ENGAGING LEARNERS

Socrates knew what captivated learners was dialogue, questions, and reflection. Mihaly Csikszentmihalyi (2008) calls it *flow*: those times that the learner is so immersed that the boundaries blur between earning a grade and finding joy in inquiry and discovery.

When learning and assessment are linked, learners track progress toward student-determined goals, have options for how to learn and display learning, make connections to real-world experiences, and utilize feedback and reflection.

Building on the ideas of engagement in Chapter 2, assessment can inherently enhance motivation by making progress visible. Like learning coding or fishing, excitement builds as progress becomes evident. In a restorative classroom, "hooking" learners leads to success.

In Practice

Ms. Gregory has been given a conventional lesson plan on simple machines (fill in your own subject: the constitution, poetry, DNA). Accompanying the lesson is a grade-level final test made up of mostly selected-choice with a few constructed responses, such as explaining the meaning of an illustration.

Standards include:

ELA: Speaking and Listening, Reading for Information, Writing (CCSS.ELA-Literacy. SL.4.1, RI.4.2, W.4.1).

Science: Plan an investigation to provide evidence of force and motion.

Essential Question: How can simple machines be used to benefit people's lives?

Combining the ideas of informative, engaging, and motivating, Ms. Gregory makes a few changes to the lesson design while honoring the standards and essential questions. She begins with a collaborative posting of incoming knowledge using sticky notes or lino. This is based on three questions:

1. Define simple machines.

2. Describe examples of simple machines.

3. Demonstrate the value of simple machines.

Images Source: **Pixabay**

She also gives an individual assessment similar to the summative assessment:

Traditional grade-level multiple-choice test questions

1. This is required to get something moving

   A. Wedge   B. Force
   C. Resistance   D. Lever

2. To reduce the amount of effort to lift something using a first class lever, move the fulcrum

   A. Closer to the   B. Closer to the
      effort   load
   C. To the center

3. The efficiency of a simple machine is always

   A. Less than 100%   B. Equal to 100%
   C. More than 100%

From the postings, she sees that levels of knowledge and understanding vary. In order to meet the reading standard, she provides two versions of Newsela (https://newsela.com) leveled readings as well as grade-appropriate videos for students to summarize in mixed groups.

To engage students and make their thinking visible, students keep a learning log throughout the unit. Their first entry is a summary of the readings. Ms. Gregory recognizes that the best readers are not always the most creative, so she decides to have students work in mixed groups on a problem:

A local engineering company wants their product purchasers to understand the value of their simple machines. Each purchase will be accompanied by an information guide that explains simple machines and promotes the purchaser's selection as the most valuable.

The requirements for this guide include:

A multimedia presentation: Student choice of platform such as PowToon, Animoto (https://animoto.com/), or emaze. Students may also provide a prototype of the machine. An alternative outcome is to create a Rube Goldberg-type tool (or illustration). Both options require citations of sources, inclusion of topical vocabulary, explanation of process/strategies used for learning and producing, and self/peer evaluation.

A running narrative of each day's progress toward the goals describes the group process, productivity, and challenges. These narratives incorporate the precise vocabulary required to understand simple machines. Each student also records his or her contribution the group's work based on guidelines for being a responsible and respectful participant. Students can also ask questions or comment privately in their daily narrative.

Throughout learning, Ms. Gregory meets regularly with each group to monitor progress; provide support, encouragement, and advice; and answer questions. Their rough draft is posted in a Google community or other safe sharing platform. Students look at the posting, ask questions, make suggestions, and provide feedback.

During the final presentations, students complete a peer evaluation using an annotated rubric that is specific to the goals and standards in the assignment.

They comment on clarity and accuracy of the ideas, the quality, comprehensiveness and helpfulness of the multimedia presentation, and reliance on source material. Ms. Gregory invites the principal to the students' final presentations. Afterward, she gives the students the grade-level final test along with the grid/table shown in Table 4.5.

TABLE 4.5 How Students Illustrate and Explain Their Learning

DRAW YOUR OWN SIMPLE MACHINE	DESCRIBE WHAT IT IS AND HOW IT WORKS	EXPLAIN HOW IT MAKES WORK EASIER	EXAMPLES IN THE REAL WORLD	ENDORSEMENT OR ADVOCACY STATEMENT
Example: Screw	An inclined plane wrapped around a shaft.	Less effort than climbing straight up the side of an object through the use of torque.	Grooves make it easier to screw into a board and hold better than a nail. Makes lug nuts easier to remove.	"Take the ramp and take it easy."
Lever				
Inclined Plane				
Wheel and Axle				
Pulley				

Image Source: Pixabay

When students see the improvement in their scores from the preassessment to the summative, they are astonished at what they have learned. Everyone moves forward with their learning, not in a lockstep manner but in an engaging, informative, safe, and personalized way.

1. What elements of personalized assessment, such as relevant, engaging, and motivational, did you see in this example?

2. How can you use some of these ideas in your own classroom and school? Think about ways to adapt traditional assessments to ones that are more personalized.

Restorative practice for learners is especially important for students who experience repeated disappointment because it supports engagement, motivation, and personalization that makes all the difference between lethargy and ownership.

> Student engagement, has been found to be predictive of a variety of desirable outcomes. Specifically, the more students are engaged in their schoolwork, the more likely they are to perform well academically, including getting higher grades in their classes, as well as higher scores on standardized tests. (Bundick, Quaglia, Corso, Haywood, 2014)

When assessment is embedded throughout learning, students make progress through small, comprehensible, and assessable steps. It is much more feasible to answer a question about the x- and y-axes after a daily lesson than to read word problems, solve equations, and show knowledge of axes, slope, intercepts, and coordinates on a summative exam.

When students set their own goals, there is greater ownership. When students contract to complete their empty outline during a teacher presentation, contribute at least one relevant comment or question each class, or complete a daily exit slip summarizing learning outcomes, it is more likely they will work toward those end points. When they know the goal can be amended, expanded, or abridged, they have a greater sense of safety, thus reducing stress and increasing willingness to work toward the goal.

When students become self-assessors, they can match their achievement to the learning intentions and in response make needed modifications. When rubrics are clear and scoring is nonjudgmental, and at the same time growth oriented, students recognize and embrace opportunities for improvement. In the course of goal setting and monitoring learning, students become more reflective and better able to utilize their emerging metacognitive skills.

As students begin to realize that assessment is not something the teacher imposes on them but rather a learning strategy to support and engage them, it becomes obvious that with practice and guidance they can improve. By removing the stress of testing, the dopamine flows more clearly and assessment becomes learning.

RECIPROCAL FEEDBACK REFOCUSES LEARNING

When assessment is a two-way street, it increases student responsibility and engagement. Lisbeth Gyllander (2012) found that when students do not understand the relationship between learning objectives, learning activities, and assessments, they are less involved in learning. A shared level of understanding increases proprietorship.

When students develop skills as goal setters and self-assessors, they become more reflective and metacognitive. When they bring their thinking and learning into the light, teachers and peers can reciprocate with analysis and feedback, and feedback leads to improvement. It is this cyclical process that provides the encouragement and support that all learners need to achieve their best.

Feedback has been studied for decades, and the specific elements of effective feedback have been widely shared. Meaningful feedback can take place between teachers and students, from student to student, or as self-assessment. Research from Ruth Butler (1988) shows that "Students given only comments scored on average 30% higher." Grades and numerical scores resulted in no gain. Grades with comments canceled the beneficial effects of comments only. This was confirmed by John Hattie (2009) who found that feedback has an effect size of 1.13, the equivalent of 1 standard deviation, confirming the belief that providing constructive and objective comments improves learning outcomes. This is especially relevant for students who have consistently had tests and papers returned with only low marks.

Feedback is a two-way street. It is the teacher who is receiving as much, if not more, information from the student as the student gets from the teacher. Moving beyond the two-way street, think of it as a traffic circle. Before the days of GPS, I remember getting stuck going around and around a traffic circle at the U.S. Capitol. I wasn't sure where I was going, found the route numbers written at each exit of the roundabout irrelevant, and had no idea how to improve my odds of success. These are the simple elements of feedback: What's my goal? How am I doing in reaching it? How can I do better? How can I help a learner get off the roundabout of learning?

Pixabay

Frequent formative assessments reinforce learning. Knowing where students are at the onset as well as routinely checking on progress throughout instruction reduces later difficulties. Think of it as a cycle of learning rather than a steep pathway directly to the pinnacle.

Reflection

In relation to feedback, what understanding and skills are most relevant in your setting? Place a 1 before those that are most important and a 2 before the ones you would like to learn more about. Then decide on the steps to take.

Add comments and clarification to your priorities.

1. _____Make feedback more of a two-way street

2. _____ Utilize reciprocal questioning to gain insight and inform responses

3. _____Provide practical and actionable guidance: Be responsive to student feedback

4. _____Explain connections to prior and future learning

5. _____Design guides to encourage and support student self-assessment

6. _____Incorporate feedback in a variety of types of learning experiences

7. _____Use student learning as feedback to my teaching

MULTIPLE PATHWAYS

If I were to ask you to show me all that you know about a topic, such as genetics, the area of a 3-dimensional object, or playing football, and you could let me know in any way you chose, what would it be? Would you prefer to write a poem, draw an illustration, make a video, or some other strategy? What if the learning intentions included three specific facts about the topic along with an accurate illustration of a key concept, or a detailed video with facts and examples?

Simply put, multiple measures mean using more than one score to make judgments about student learning. Of course, one reading test cannot tell us our students' reading level any more than a standardized test can be used to judge a teacher's ability. Multiple measures are more likely to sample a range of students' knowledge, cognitive abilities, and performance skills. They also help us make better decisions about achievement and interventions. Rafe can tell me a dozen interesting things he has read in a biography, but he hates to read Charles Dickens and becomes inattentive when it is the required reading.

FLEXIBLE ASSESSMENT IS PERSONAL ASSESSMENT

The word *flexible* is especially relevant to at-risk learners. As with many topics in assessment, there are contrasting perspectives, from the belief that all students, with very few exceptions, should be taking normalized tests to the opposite end of the spectrum where every student requires a personal assessment plan. Common sense is found somewhere in the middle, where research and theory inform practice.

Assessment is dependent on students' academic competencies and individual attributes. As such, the need for flexibility and modifications vary. How many ways can you think of to show what you know about the meaning of Einstein's theory of relativity or the plot of Shakespeare's *Cymbeline*? What if science were as easy to understand as Lin-Manual Miranda has made history with his musical production of *Hamilton*? More important, why can't it be?

FLEXIBLE AND CONSISTENT

Carol Ann Tomlinson and Tonya Moon (2013) explain that it is essential to

> take into account both the student's needs and the requirements of the assessment situation. In most instances it is possible to accommodate student needs by viewing the context as flexible as feasible. (p. 426)

With flexible assessment the standards are consistent, but what varies is the process for achieving them and the ways students show their achievement. Sue Rieg (2007) found that

> students who share in the assessment process perceive more control of, and more responsibility for, their learning; therefore, students can, and should help to determine the criteria by which their work will be judged as this gives students a feeling of empowerment and makes evaluation feel less punitive (Brookhart, 1997; Kohn, 1993). (Discussion section, para. 1).

DIVERGENT ROUTES

The National Science Standard of "Examining the human impact on earth's systems, gathering credible information, and designing solutions" has the potential for flexible assessments and multiple approaches. Students may research and advocate for the reinstatement of the Civilian Conservation Corps or, alternatively, urge others to donate trees because planting them is good for the environment. Others may develop a blueprint for an ecofriendly community garden or write an editorial on the importance of sustainable forestry. With each outcome, there are consistent criteria: Explain the evidence of human impact on resources, effects of using nonrenewable resources, and planning ways to monitor and minimize human impact on the environment.

In Mr. Samash's class, students research topics of interest to them. The research project has common requirements such as use of effective research strategies (that is, search queries, source checking, evaluation of diverse perspectives, synthesis of critical facts and ideas). The students, classmates, and teacher annotate and evaluate their learning using a rubric. Students then write "test" questions about their individual and small-group presentations. One group decides to write multiple-choice questions:

Scientists suggest that growing more trees will help slow down the process of global warming because

1. Trees add bacteria to the soil

2. Trees absorb excess carbon dioxide from the atmosphere

3. Trees remove excess water from the soil

4. Trees feed nutrients back into the soil

Another group writes a completion question:

Which gas is released during photosynthesis? _____

A third group asks the students to circle and correct the three errors in this statement:

> Cutting down trees helps slow down global warming. Nucleoids capture the energy from sunlight and convert it to energy for the plant. Tree limbs absorb the water that plants and trees need to survive.

In addition to the students' written questions, the test takers write rhymes, poems, raps, or fables (reference Dr. Seuss, haiku, Æsop). They are required to include a specified number of identified vocabulary and key concepts to express their learning. Scoring is based on clarity of the explanation and accuracy of use. Sirah writes this adaptation of a cinquain and notes the definitions below it.

Tree Roots

Shallow, Hungry

Water, Air, Nutrients

Deprived, Hollow

Dead

This type of flexibility in assessment gives students choice and voice in demonstrating learning while maintaining common standards and consistent learning outcomes. As always, the emphasis is on growth toward mastery.

CHOICE

Choice builds a sense of empowerment that in turn fosters confidence. Ericka Patall, Harris Cooper, and Jorgianne Robinson (2008) found a connection between choice, intrinsic motivation, effort, and learning outcomes. This connection is strongest when the following criteria are met:

- The choices need to be relevant to the learning outcomes and instruction.

- Choice needs to be meaningful to the learner's goals and interests.

- Choice is a routine part of teaching and learning.

- However, irrelevant extrinsic rewards are not effective.

Choice boards are used by many teachers to connect choices to levels of the taxonomy. They also give significance and clarity to the learning. For example, students developing mastery of a new language may be provided with choices that build content vocabulary. Students who meet the vocabulary standard, in addition to vocabulary building, are also expected to identify synonyms and antonyms or complete an analysis of the vocabulary in a specific context. For more advanced learners, choices include higher-level evaluation and production of original ideas. Table 4.6 shows an example of a choice board in a third-grade class.

TABLE 4.6 Assessment Choice

VOCABULARY DEVELOPMENT	VOCABULARY EXPANSION	VOCABULARY MASTERY
Write down the vocabulary words and then compose an original sentence using them.	Write a letter explaining the vocabulary to someone who has no experience with it.	Create a graphic organizer/mind map that adds more descriptive and complex words to the basic vocabulary.
Match vocabulary to illustrations. Explain your thinking.	EdPuzzle: Watch the video. Record and evaluate the use of the content vocabulary in helping the viewer understand the meaning.	Produce a video tutorial on the content vocabulary. Include examples to expand the viewer's understanding.
Quizlet or Quizizz: Review vocabulary in a multiple-choice quiz format.	Create flash cards with synonyms or illustrations of the vocabulary.	Write a short story that shows your understanding of the terminology.

Essential principles of choice:

1. Offer choices that are reasonable for students and teacher, time, setting, and resources.

2. Align options with the learning intentions.

3. Include opportunities for all learners to be successful.

4. Invite students to develop and amplify some choices.

5. Include reasonable limits.

6. Be specific in writing directions.

7. Explicitly explain success criteria.

8. Adjust the number of choices as appropriate.

RESTORING ASSESSMENT THROUGH FLEXIBILITY, DIVERGENCE, CHOICE, AND VOICE

In relation to assessment, flexibility is especially important for at-risk learners. Personalization leads to a "no excuses" classroom where students make purposeful choices that protect and support their own interests, safety, and welfare. Every type of assessment has benefits and drawbacks, but when students can select one that is most relevant, each one discovers the best way to provide evidence of their learning. Flexibility and choice are essential in a restorative classroom because they reduce antagonism and support diversity. Risk and stress are reduced as learners develop a sense of competency throughout learning rather than relying on a single final score. If equity is the goal, then students must be able to demonstrate their abilities in ways that make sense to them.

Strategies for Giving Students Choice and Voice

1. Verify that the learning goals and success criteria are consistent for each student and that the assessment is measuring the planned and taught learning intentions; then make the necessary modifications.

2. Select an alternative location to complete the assessment that has less distractions.

3. Provide additional tools—for example, yardsticks, sticky notes, or technology.

4. Be flexible with use of time.

5. If it is a teacher-designed test, align the questions with the sequence of learning, from the lower levels of the taxonomy to higher ones. Indicate a stopping point for specific students that you know will quickly reach their frustration level. As needed, provide alternative work for them while other students complete the assessment.

6. Weigh different parts of the assessment in ways that align with students' strengths. One student may do well with multiple choice, while another will do better if she can complete a prompt.

7. Incorporate real-world connections to engage students in ways that are meaningful to them.

8. Deconstruct math word problems to number problems or vice versa.

9. Some students may need to take variable pathways toward achievement. Madir may need to have the book right next to him, while others can use their more developed levels of recall.

10. Let students choose a question or problem from multiple levels of an assignment, such as building knowledge, applying learning, demonstrating mastery.

11. Not all students are successful with all types of measures. Ramadji may require a word bank for completion items, while Janessa needs to have the length of the essay reduced or to answer it orally.

12. Give students the opportunity to decide how to summarize their learning. Maintain rigor by requiring specific levels of the taxonomy in their summaries, such as review of key points, application of ideas, synthesis of ideas, and lingering questions.

13. While aiming for consistent standards, recognize that there are multiple ways for students to demonstrate proficiency.

14. Reporting may need to be adjusted for students who are mastering lower grade-level standards yet demonstrating progress.

15. Growth measures and indications of improvement are best for those students who are striving toward mastery of grade-level standards.

16. Incorporate self-assessment based on the standards, success criteria, and scoring instruments that were explained at the start of learning.

17. Engage students in responding to their summative assessment grade: Explain what they got wrong and what they now understand, determine a way to clarify any misunderstandings (research, reading, ask an expert), and briefly summarize how this changed their thinking.

Reflection

How can you use these ideas to adjust and upskill your own assessment practices?

How can you personalize assessment yet focus on consistent progress toward standards?

How can you provide choice so that all students can be successful?

Select two of the strategies for making assessment flexible and explain how you would like to use them.

1.

2.

Add your own strategies for making assessment flexible and giving students choice and voice.

1.

2.

CHAPTER 5

Reconsidering Noncognitive Skills

Chapter Goals/Key Ideas

Noncognitive skills are important: Incorporate them throughout teaching and learning.

There is a strong connection between noncognitive attributes and life achievement.

Mastery of noncognitive skills and dispositions is essential for at-risk learners.

There is both rationale and strategy for assessing noncognitive skills and attributes.

COGNITIVE AND NONCOGNITIVE: NOT AN EITHER/OR

iStock.com/bayhayalet

Emerging research shows that cognitive competencies are built on foundations of social, emotional, and personal attributes. According to the Institute of Education, "Non-cognitive skills including self-control and engagement in learning are correlated with high academic outcomes" (Gutman & Schoon, 2013, p. 2). In these schools, educators and students embrace, scale up, and utilize these building blocks.

Call them what you like, metacognitive, noncognitive, social-emotional, or something else, they are the keystones that support academic achievement. Church builders in the twelfth century learned that if the keystone wasn't stable, the building would collapse. While these foundations are important for all learners, they are essential in restorative settings for vulnerable students.

There are numerous measures of cognitive outcomes, from standardized tests to textbook test banks. Typically, these produce numerical data on academic learning. It is also possible to make noncognitive-cognitive skills visible. From minute-by-minute check-ins in the classroom to more standardized measures, the value of understanding each student's noncognitive frames is fundamental to success.

The ingenuity of underserved learners has always astonished me. Maybe they have learned to maneuver around a system that categorizes them, or perhaps they live in a world where being flexible and resourceful best meets their needs. As Albert Einstein reminds us, "Not everything that counts can be counted, and not everything that can be counted counts."

SKILLS AND DISPOSITIONS FOR SUCCESS

Students from diverse socioeconomic and cultural groups bring distinct skills, traditions, and perceptions to the classroom. Whatever you may believe is at the heart of these variations, it influences each child's educational attainment. For children who begin school academically behind their more privileged peers, the challenges may continue throughout their educational narrative.

While academic interventions have proven effective to some extent, it is also feasible and essential to modify skills and dispositions in order to sustain success. Many of these attributes are malleable and teachable within the daily routines of learning. Rosen, Glennie, Dalton, Lennon, and Boznik (2010) explain in their summary of research on seven major noncognitive skills that

> noncognitive attributes and skills may play an important role in reversing or limiting delays or deficiencies in cognitive development and academic achievement. They may complement direct efforts to improve academic learning. (p. 9)

Skills are different than knowledge-based learning in that they emphasize ways, means, and habits of learning. Students can learn how to purposefully use these essential abilities such as

- planning,

- goal orientation,

- time management,

- study strategies,

- effective communication,

- collaboration,

- problem solving,

- metacognition, and

- higher-order thinking such as analyzing, evaluating, and creating.

Hattie and Donoghue (2016) emphasize the importance of embedding and building the skills within the context of learning, and accentuate the value of aligning them with the learning goals and tasks.

Dispositions influence how students approach and engage in learning. Many dispositions are timeless and universal.

While studies of early temperament explain that babies are born quiet or boisterous, shy or sociable, flexible or slow to warm up, most of these traits are variable and malleable throughout childhood. If you watch the *Babies* (Chabat, Rouxel, & Billot, 2010) documentary, the cultural variations in child rearing and the commonalities in achieving developmental landmarks are evident.

Learning dispositions include these and many more. (Note that the word *attributes* is used interchangeably with *dispositions* in this chapter.)

- Self-efficacy

- Perspective-taking

- Personal responsibility

- Purposeful perseverance

- Conscientiousness

- Motivation

- Resilience

- Learning from mistakes

- Curiosity

- Self-regulation

Keep in mind that dispositions can be situational. There are times that children can see the light at the end of the learning tunnel, and other times when their self-control is challenged by overwhelming doubt or loss of trust. Developing these emerging frames of learning is where schools *can* make a difference in amplifying student success.

The research from Carol Dweck (2007) on mindset, Angela Duckworth (2016) on grit, Camille Farrington (2013) on academic mindsets and deeper learning, and Mary Helen Immordino-Yang (2015) on emotions and learning all deepen our understanding of their development, role, and value. Research on the roots of emotions, personality, and character indeed go deep, but for some reason, in the classroom there is a belief that if the teacher just teaches better, chooses this or that packaged program, or uses the just-right learning management system, test scores will improve.

Caveat: As my good friend and psychologist Josephine Beebe taught me, a weakness can be a strength that is overused. For example, a person can push the envelope of a strength such as determination to the extreme of hard-headedness. If we overdo personal responsibility, it can lead to feelings of guilt.

Reflection

The listing of skills and dispositions is emergent. For now:

1. What skills are most important to you, your students, and your setting?

2. Which are strong now, and which do you want to develop?

3. What dispositions are most important to you, your students, and your setting?

4. Which are strong now, and which do you want to develop?

THE IMPORTANCE OF NONCOGNITIVE SKILLS AND DISPOSITIONS

As schools continue to emphasize academic knowledge, and teachers struggle to improve the mandated learning outcomes, in many settings the arts, career, and life skills have been reduced or eliminated. Yet our graduates' test scores remain relatively stagnant. Teaching harder has not been proven to raise achievement.

Rather, there is increasing evidence that nonacademic social-emotional skills and strategies contribute to the foundations of academic achievement as well as success in life. "A growing body of empirical research shows that non-cognitive skills rival IQ in predicting education attainment, workplace success, health, and criminality" (Kautz, Heckman, Diris, Weel, & Borghans, 2014, p. 10).

There is adequate evidence that extrinsic motivation does not work in the long term. Perhaps you can get a student to take a test by offering candy, but the next time, you will have to offer a bigger incentive. Typically, this will only work in the short term. As Susan Headden and Sarah McKay (2015) explain, "When rewards come to be expected, they can have the effect of undermining motivation in general and intrinsic motivation in particular" (p. 7).

Higher-order thinking is more apt to be strengthened by and demonstrated through purposeful and rigorous projects and extended performance tasks. These multifaceted assignments require complex thinking that is amplified by noncognitive skills and dispositions. This, in turn, requires insightful assessment of problem solving, goal monitoring, and self-regulation. Students are more likely to develop these underlying intrinsic skills when they have reasonable and relevant choices, are supported as independent learners, and given a feasible rationale for what they are doing.

Noncognitive for At-Risk Learners

Many factors make students vulnerable: persistent failure, bullying, stress, family pressures, isolation, disorganization, disconnection, discrimination, apathy, helplessness, discouragement, real or perceived threats, and boredom. Children who face adversity, whether it is linguistic, cultural, familial, or socioeconomic, also face challenges in nutrition, housing, health, and resources. The development of a sense of safety and belonging, the foundation of Maslow's (1943, 1954) Hierarchy of Needs, must be met before anyone can attain higher levels of self-worth, dignity, and personal achievement.

CASE STUDY

Ms. Falconi's class this year includes a diverse group of speakers of other languages, transient, neglected, and overwhelmed. Ms. Falconi agrees with Gutman and Schoon's (2013) explanation that

> children's perception of their ability, their expectations of future success, and the extent to which they value an activity influences their motivation. Persistence leads to improved academic outcomes, especially for low-attaining pupils. (p. 2)

She believes that she can make a difference through her focus on noncognitive attributes. She knows that success comes from an inner drive that is based on a complex mix of tenacity, autonomy, interest, goal orientation, reasonable challenge, choice, relevance, and belonging. She also knows that for at-risk students, the development of these traits may be weaker due to prior experience with failure, lack of resources, and concerns about personal safety. She read about and confers with other teachers on strategies and models for preparing these students academically, socially, and emotionally for the world beyond the classroom. Combined with her own experience, workshops, and readings, she adopts these eight systemic approaches to teaching, learning, and assessing.

1. NURTURE RELATIONSHIPS

Relationships are the cornerstone of learning. When learning is based on mutual trust and respect, students know that someone has their back. A concerned teacher or caring adult can make a big difference in students' engagement and achievement. In turn, these feelings build personal dispositions such as empathy and self-efficacy. Within these positive and encouraging environments, students are more likely to be motivated to learn and less likely to accept failure as the norm.

Mutuality and respect are a foundation of good relationships. When Ms. Falconi says to Taywan and Sharma, "I would get frustrated too with the grade on your project. Let's figure out what we can do to help you work together to share the learning load more equitably and reorganize the sequence of your work. Then we'll ask the class to let you present your ideas again," they recognize this as an opportunity to improve performance.

When Taywan and Sharma are part of a learning community, they are more apt to have a sense of belonging. When students feel they have someone who cares about them, they are better able to respond to misunderstandings and mistakes as a normal part of learning. Purposefully grouping students by mixed ability with peer support or by same ability with focused support, for example, can help the students feel more accepted and respected. As Peter Elbow (as cited in Fried, 2001) says,

> surely we are incomplete as teachers if we are committed only to what we are teaching but not to our students, or only to our students but not to what we are teaching, or halfhearted in our commitment to both. (p. 51)

2. DEVELOP SELF-REGULATION

Kathleen Vohs and Roy Baumeister (2012) have studied self-control and willpower for several decades and note that people perform relatively poorly on tests of self-control when they have engaged in previous situations requiring significant self-control. They discovered that this depletion of willpower is especially relevant in at-risk populations who more frequently face difficult choices, have little emotional capital, and cope with persistent frustration and situations they have little control over.

Rather than teaching everyone generic self-control strategies, it is more effective to help students identify their hot buttons and in response develop focused avenues to management. For Wallace, recognizing that by the end of the morning he has difficulty staying on task or being patient with others means that he can manage these feelings and behaviors by removing himself from the group to work in a quiet corner of the room. For Felicia, when Ramona persistently bothers her at lunchtime, she knows she can choose a different place to eat and gain control by preventing the issue until they both can get guidance on solving this ongoing problem. Marcus, who gets anxious when papers are being returned, knows he can ask the teacher to return his first while he is still calm enough to review the feedback and figure out what to do next.

3. FOSTER A GROWTH MINDSET

Dweck and Leggett (1988) report that positive learning dispositions can be developed with practice. "Students with a fixed mindset believe that their intellectual ability is a limited entity, and they tend to worry about proving it rather than improving it" (p. 258). They are more apt to feel dumb, embarrassed, and easily frustrated, resulting in giving up more easily. Students with a growth mindset believe that they can improve their abilities with work and practice. This in turn leads to a willingness to learn from missteps, consider alternative approaches, and take on new challenges.

From the research on mindset comes recommendations for strategies that support the development of a growth mindset. Praising effort and improvement rather than intelligence is a critical element. Telling students that their determination paid off while concurrently ensuring that goals and assignments are achievable is essential. Breaking down work into smaller portions and sequencing it from easier to increasingly difficult can help students climb each rung of the learning ladder, one step at a time.

What the experts say about mindset:

> Mangels, Butterfield, Lamb, Good, and Dweck (2006) found that different regions of the brain are associated with different mindsets. "When reviewing a solution to a question they had answered incorrectly, students with a growth mindset displayed greater activation of brain regions associated with deep semantic processing" (p. 11). This suggests that they were acknowledging their mistake and trying to learn from it. Indeed, activation in this brain region predicted better performance on a later test.

> Blackwell, Trzesniewski, and Dweck (2007) explain that teaching students that intelligence is malleable and providing them with strategies for shaping their intelligence resulted in higher performance in math from the beginning to the end of the school year. Teaching memory devices such as mnemonics and motivational routines such as self-talk as well as celebrating mistakes as steps toward resolution and growth can support this mindset.

After Ms. Falconi presents the big-picture goal, she works with students to deconstruct and make it more reasonable and relevant. She starts by asking them to lift something heavy, and then explains that today their brains will be doing the heavy lifting. She reminds them of a time that they learned something really hard, such as making foul shots, and then works with them to break down the upcoming learning task as they did the athletic task: effort, balance, focus, release, and so forth. She then has them do a similar process with the learning goal.

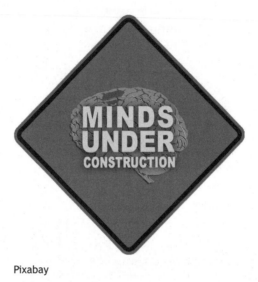

Pixabay

4. ENCOURAGE LEARNING AND ASSESSMENT OF COMPETENCY, MASTERY, AND GROWTH

The ideas and ideals of mastery learning explained in Chapter 3 also apply to the development of noncognitive skills and dispositions. When students follow achievable progressions and see evidence of progressive mastery, they are more willing to work toward the next level. When giving high-stakes tests or routine assessments, be sure the sequence of questions and tasks align with the sequence of the learning progression.

This could mean that they know the vocabulary, understand the concept, label the steps to achievement, and recognize success indicators. Using the examples in Chapter 3, Ms. Falconi develops a rubric that aligns with the grade-level math progression. The unit test is sequenced to match this progression of competency:

1. Recognize fractions as numbers

2. Understand fractions as the quantity formed by partition of a whole

3. Represent fractions on a number line

4. Explain equivalent fractions

5. Compare two fractions with the same numerator or denominator

In class, learning begins with the whole class labeling halves and quarters on the interactive board and then in small groups solving word problems. This is followed by working with a partner to partition number lines, and lastly, to express fraction equivalents. Once Amala and her teacher determine her level of mastery, she stops answering the progressively sequenced questions on the unit test at her personal level of frustration and reverts to a tutorial to build her skills toward the next level. Doing so helps students avoid outbursts of frustration and reminds them that learning is sequential.

5. MAKE LEARNING AND ASSESSMENT MEANINGFUL AND RELEVANT

When my daughter was in fourth grade, she came home from school on testing day and said she did not complete the essay part of the standardized test. When asked why, she sighed, "What do I know about building a playground in an alleyway?" In contrast to my urban upbringing, she had grown up in a semirural community where playgrounds were open fields with an occasional slide or swing set. Now put yourself in the shoes of a child with a different historical narrative and no experience with Dr. Seuss's rhymes, recipes, fractions, using credit, or farm life. Keep in mind that a single misunderstood word in a question can reduce students' success significantly: amoral versus immoral, and bazaar versus bizarre.

Students embrace learning that has meaning for them. Rather than summarizing a reading in science, ask students how the topic, whether it be density or division, connects to their lives. Ask them to consider how the issues in a local election can change their community, or to compare and contrast Shakespeare's *Othello* and the movie *O*. Relevance is an important element of assessment and can be achieved by providing high task authenticity.

As Ms. Falconi plans meaningful assessment, she considers the clarity of the content, rationale for learning, the levels of thinking required, the relevance to students' lives, and flexibility in showing what they know. She asks them to contribute to the test design and provides opportunities to annotate their answers and occasions for personal application, self-assessment, reflection, and questioning.

6. EXPLICITLY TEACH NONCOGNITIVE SKILLS

Robyn Collins (2014) recommends teaching "not only the language and concepts, but also telling students . . . what skills they are exercising and the level of complexity of the question or problem" (p. 14). Include this in test questions by asking students to explain how they used recall to answer a question, whether they are applying or analyzing when completing an experiment, or how persistence is helping them move forward.

Students can be taught strategies for mastering noncognitive skills by explaining how they are transferring learning from one situation to another, or what they learned from a previous mistake. Students can learn to recognize the elements of creativity through an analysis of the work of creative people they admire. They can annotate the steps in problem solving that the Little Prince or Harry Potter used, or keep a log of how they used self-regulation to cope with particularly frustrating situations.

Ms. Falconi knows that learning self-regulation and self-reliance comes in small steps. Antwan may be dismayed at this test grade, but tracking the improvement from prior scores to the current ones can help him remain more composed and optimistic. Skills such as counting to five, stretching, or taking a deep breath before acting on impulse can also be taught and strengthened. She reminds him to think about the things he is good at, such as soccer or consoling his friends, and also encourages self-regulation. This helps him recognize the value of what he has mastered and make connections to the learning of more complex skills. Movies based on strong and real-life role models such as those in *The Pursuit of Happyness* help children recognize what it takes to overcome life's obstacles.

The example shown in Table 5.1 gives students an opportunity to analyze the errors they made and also provides guidance on ways to fix them.

TABLE 5.1   Metacognition on Mistakes

ASSIGNMENT OR QUESTION #	DIDN'T UNDERSTAND THE ASSIGNMENT OR QUESTION BECAUSE . . .	I MADE THIS SIMPLE MISTAKE	NEED MORE TIME OR PRACTICE	NEED MORE TEACHER-DIRECTED INSTRUCTION	THIS IS WAY TOO HARD BECAUSE
1.					
2.					
3.					
Comments					

7. UTILIZE EFFECTIVE LEARNING STRATEGIES

Learning strategies can connect cognitive and noncognitive learning. They support the ambiguity of deeper thinking or provide insights into one's personal construction of meaning. Hattie and Donoghue (2016) propose that "various learning strategies are more powerful and better connected to certain steps in the learning cycle" (p. 1).

Some students need additional specificity and support. When students know their strengths and can choose how they show learning, they kindle a growth mindset that leads to a personal belief in success. For example, Adina writes a letter to the editor on how cuts to the local school budget will affect her education, while LaQuil produces a video in which he interviews other students, teachers, and his principal, and then summarizes their ideas.

Students can self-regulate learning when the expected outcomes are clear and the steps are practical and manageable. Throughout the process, they record and explain their progress, ask questions, and ponder lingering gaps. Documented learning maps, annotated learning plans, and graphic organizers can support even the most disorganized students and lead to better strategies for managing time and resources. Ms. Falconi has designed an annotated math plan as shown in Table 5.2.

TABLE 5.2   Student Annotated Math Learning Plan

LEARNING GOAL	HERE'S WHAT I UNDERSTAND IN MY OWN WORDS	HERE ARE EXAMPLES OF WHAT I CAN DO	I STILL HAVE QUESTIONS ABOUT
I can convert measurements in a larger unit into a smaller unit using the same system of measures.			
I can record measurement equivalents in a two-column table.			
I can use the four operations to solve word problems that involve distance, time, volume, and money.			
I can represent measurement quantities using diagrams.			
Teacher's annotations and feedback.			

8. CULTIVATE CREATIVITY

Some of my most creative students aren't the ones who are academically successful. I recognized that it was important to embrace their creative talents while simultaneously holding them accountable for learning. In an upper grade level in Ms. Falconi's district, Mr. Ianolo wants to be sure the requirements of the assignment align with the goals of the unit:

1. Analyze the causes of the Civil War.

2. Describe the major turning point/battles.

3. Elaborate on the day-to-day life and experiences of a soldier.

4. Analyze significant speeches and proclamations.

5. Synthesize the outcomes and effects of the war.

Maria wanted to write a novella about the Civil War instead of analyzing the politics and events of the war. Her story was told through the eyes of an eleven-year-old white girl and her black maid growing up during the war years. In her story, she used multiple viewpoints to discuss the causes, events, speeches, daily life, and outcomes of the war.

Students can be afraid to show their creative side, whether it is because they would be labeled as different or think they can't align their creative ideas to the standards and learning outcomes. While it may not work for every subject and unit, it is possible to engage disenfranchised students through their creativity. Give students opportunities to brainstorm solutions to problems; use a problem-solving process and show them how to question deeply with "what if" and "why not" questions.

Creativity is teachable and assessable. Elements of creativity include curiosity by wanting to know how things work, fluency in producing a number of solutions, flexibility in looking at conventional things in new ways, and elaboration to improve existing ideas. Rather than simply labeling shapes, elementary students can go on a shape hunt in their school and then incorporate and label the shapes of things in their drawings of the school. Older students can add and label bones and/or organs to a drawing of themselves. Students can self-assess their creativity and subsequently develop a plan to strengthen those powers.

In the real world, the ability to generate new ideas and solve problems in innovative ways is a valuable skill. Yet in education, convergent thinking and the idea of seeking the one right answer is most valued. Encourage divergent thinking in your classroom by giving students an answer and then asking how many ways they can pose the question or problem. Ask second graders about the meaning of the answer 100, and ask fourth graders how sizzle, hiccup, and meow are similar. In middle school, students can come up with five ways to solve a problem, rate each for its originality or feasibility, and then have peers do the same. High school students can explain ways to harness the clouds or explain diversity to a clone who is going to teach others.

SUMMARY: THE CASE FOR NONCOGNITIVE

The idea of academic tenacity that promotes long-term learning and achievement has been described by Dweck, Walton, and Cohen (2014) as "the skills that allow students to look beyond short-term concerns to longer-term or higher-order goals, and withstand challenges and setbacks to persevere toward these goals" (p. 4).

There is emerging evidence of a correlation between noncognitive skills such as academic tenacity and academic performance. It is important to note that although self-control and perseverance have been shown to have a positive relationship to successful academic outcomes, "these skills are inter-related and need to be developed in combination with each other" (Gutman & Schoon, 2013, p. 2).

In today's world, we don't need people who excel at Trivial Pursuit or can name all of Shakespeare's plays. Rather, we need curious lifelong learners who seek to deeply understand situations, consider multiple ideas, seek continuous growth, are flexible and resourceful, and can adapt to changes in the world around them.

Reflection

When Glorita is asked about the possibility of eating a hamburger as big as an elephant, she says that she couldn't imagine doing that. With a little prompting to her imagination, such as eating an elephant-sized fried potato or a giant peach, she recognized the analogy and decided to ask for a knife and fork. Rolando asked for a shrinking machine.

Since it is not possible to exercise all the skills and dispositions at once, start by selecting the two or three from Table 5.3 that are most relevant or most essential in your setting. Then identify steps you can take to help students move forward with that strategy.

TABLE 5.3 Pathways to Noncognitive Skills

STRATEGIES FOR NONCOGNITIVE SUCCESS	PATHWAY TO ACTION
1. Building Relationships	
2. Developing Self-Regulation	
3. Fostering a Growth Mindset	
4. Encouraging Learning and Assessment for Competency, Mastery, and Growth	
5. Making Learning and Assessment Meaningful and Relevant	
6. Explicit Teaching of Noncognitive Skills	
7. Utilizing Effective Learning Strategies	
8. Cultivating Creativity	

ASSESSING NONCOGNITIVE SKILLS AND DISPOSITIONS

Wordle.com

Noncognitive skills are precursors to the success of students in school and beyond. Jones, Greenberg, and Crowley (2015) found "statistically significant association between measured social-emotional skills in kindergarten and key young adult outcomes across multiple domains of education, employment, criminal activity, substance use, and mental health" (p. 1). Emerging evidence shows they are essential to life success, but when it comes to assessing them, there are arguments on both sides of the aisle. In nurturing and sustaining those more vulnerable learners, noncognitive skills are essential in restoring their dignity, drive, and outlook.

Noncognitive skills are not new. The ancients knew about morality, self-regulation, and character. Today, they have numerous names: social-emotional learning, executive function, metacognition, and learning styles. They are also described as tempera-ments, personality traits, and Habits of Mind (Costa & Kallick, 2008). Heckman and Kautz (2012) call them "Soft Skills."

Research shows that noncognitive skills emerge developmentally, similar to cogni-tive skills, and are similarly influenced by the environment. Neuroscientists explain that learning passes through the amygdala, within our limbic system, at the brain's emotional hub. If emotionality, relationships, and intrapersonal dispositions are important for learning, then they are certainly worth teaching and shaping. And if they are worth teaching, they are worth assessing.

Traditionally, these noncognitive skills and dispositions have not been measured by standardized tests. Some believe they cannot be tested due to questions of validity and reliability. Others argue that standards and benchmarks for them haven't been accurately and fully developed and tested. Educators are concerned that they will be used to evaluate teacher and school performance, but that doesn't preclude using noncognitive assessments for other purposes.

In 1948, Henry Chauncey, the first president of Educational Testing Service (ETS; SAT and GRE tests) sought to promote the assessment of

> personal qualities, some of which may be drive, motivation, conscientious-ness, intellectual stamina . . . the ability to get along with others . . . and interests, such as aesthetic, religious, social, economic, political. (Lemann, 1995, p. 84, cited in Kyllonen, 2005)

This led to the establishment of the ETS personality research group in the 1960s. But with the advent of Title I and standardized testing, these ideas were moved to the back burner. Interest is being rekindled, and methods to measure noncognitive and social-emotional learning are being developed. Here are a few current examples

---

Stanford University's Project for Education Research that Scales (PERTS) is based on a 6-point Likert scale for self-reporting mindset, perseverance, and learning dispositions.

ETS: High School Success Navigator assesses skills correlated with achievement.

CASEL, the Collaborative for Academic, Social, and Emotional Learning, is working with various states to create developmentally sensitive standards emphasizing five competencies: self-awareness, self-management, social awareness, relationship skills, and responsible decision making.

University of Bristol Effective Lifelong Learning Inventory uses a 4-point Likert scale to identify learning preferences and capacities such as curiosity, creativity, and resilience.

Behavioral Analytics track learners as they learn by recording time spent on task and facial expressions indicating tenacity, response to frustration, and reward-seeking.

PISA (Program for International Student Assessment) offers students a questionnaire about their self-efficacy, self-esteem, and relationships with teachers.

The Gallup Student Poll, YouthTruth, and California's CORE are other systems developing assessments of students' social and emotional outlook and actions.

It will take some time before these assessments are validated and precise enough for classroom use. In the meantime, there are strategies that teachers can use in the classroom to engage learners in developing and assessing noncognitive dispositions and recognizing their importance.

Reflection

1. Where do you stand on the value of assessing noncognitive skills? Consider the benefits and risks in your reflection.

2. Note on the line below those skills that you feel should definitely be assessed and those you don't. Include an explanation as relevant.

Definitely   Maybe   Never

_____

Elaborate on your analysis:

Example

Definitely: Mindset, because it affects a student's outlook on learning and is malleable/teachable.

Maybe: Social awareness, because norms can vary between cultures.

Socioeconomic achievement gaps have been identified in academics, specifically in relation to testable knowledge-based learning outcomes. But what would happen if we were to assess all students on noncognitive attributes such as perseverance, flexibility, or problem solving? Is it possible that students who perform poorly on standardized tests would score equally well or better than their more advantaged peers? Consider how creative the people of Cuba became when they only had automobiles from the 1950s yet needed basic transportation. Doesn't music encourage resilience with songs like "We Shall Overcome," "Let it Go," and "I Hope You Dance?" What if you asked your class to create a rap about perseverance, like this one written by a student: "Sticking to a plan of action is to persevere, you can fully reach your goals when you're an imagineer."

It may not be a good idea to hold schools, teachers, districts, and states accountable for students' noncognitive skills, but it is a good idea to help students recognize how valuable they are in personal success and to help them build those foundations. Consider the potential and possibilities for using information about self-esteem and feelings of connectedness in the classroom.

How would you go about assessing students' noncognitive skills? Would you give them the National Assessment of Educational Progress noncognitive instrument or an online assessment from Mindset Works? Would you meet face-to-face and ask the student questions, or maybe have them respond to case studies or tales of morality? Perhaps their responses would help you understand how they typically react to anger, boredom, or setbacks. Alternatively, consider developing a customized set of questions where students indicate their level of agreement or disagreement on a Likert scale. There are no right or wrong answers but rather opportunities for reflection and modification. Here are some ideas to help you get started.

1. Academic Skills

   A. My brainpower is a basic part of me and can't be changed very much.

   B. I prefer to be told what I am expected to learn and be guided in learning it.

   C. To be successful, I often use learning strategies such as taking smaller steps.

   D. I get nervous and have really negative thoughts about taking tests.

   E. Learning is exciting; I love finding new facts and thinking about new ideas.

2. Achievement Dispositions

   A. The harder you work at learning something, the better you become.

   B. I am able to keep working toward the end goal as I solve a problem.

   C. I see the things I do in school as irrelevant to me.

   D. If I do poorly on a test or assignment, it must be my fault.

   E. Talents and aptitudes such as music or athletics can be learned by anyone.

3. Self-Regulation

   A. I like learning, even when I have to work at it.

   B. When I get frustrated, I give up easily.

   C. It is so easy for me to get distracted.

   D. I agree with this quote: "The road to success is paved with hard work."

   E. If I am left alone to work on an assignment, I quickly lose interest.

4. Social Connections

   A. I learn a lot when I work with others to solve problems.

   B. I feel like I fit in with my classmates.

   C. I know that help is available should I need it.

   D. I am a rugged individualist when it comes to school work.

   E. I don't like to speak up in class because someone might make fun of me.

Students may annotate each section with an explanation of their rating or a change they would like to make. Use that to initiate a discussion about situations in which the feeling or awareness is most likely to occur and how to respond to it. This can also lead to a sharing of ideas about how to change one's outlook and reactions. Alternatively, use stories about empathy, case studies about courage, images about despair, an activity like the marshmallow test, or video using PlayPosit to gain insights into students' noncognitive thinking.

In addition to the assessments of noncognitive skills, there are gauges of learning styles worth exploring, such as Howard Gardner's Multiple Intelligences, Witkin's Field-Dependence/Independence, Devereux Student Strengths Assessment, Gregorc's Style Delineator, or Myers-Briggs Type Indicator.

FORMATIVE IN SUPPORT OF NONCOGNITIVE

Taking the assessment of noncognitive skills and dispositions to the next step means using the information and data that are generated. Standardized assessments are used for ranking students, comparing schools, rating teachers, and long-term tracking. Assessment of noncognitive skills, by nature, have divergent purposes:

1. Help students understand the beliefs and behaviors underlying their learning and thinking.

2. Build the skills and dispositions that strengthen learning outcomes.

3. Recognize behaviors that may interfere with success.

4. Provide actionable interventions in redirecting those behaviors.

5. Adjust teaching and learning to best meet the needs of all learners.

6. Explicitly teach skills for success.

7. Support students in reaching higher levels of more complex learning.

8. Recognize and acknowledge changes to students' skills and dispositions with experience and time.

In Chapter 2, formative assessment is defined as a purposeful process used by teachers and students during learning that provides actionable feedback to guide and inform adjustments to teaching and learning with the aim of improving learning outcomes. Formative assessment is not a strategy but rather a process that relies on multiple approaches for gathering information about learning. In response, the teacher and students work together to identify the best way to respond to students' mistakes, misjudgments, or misunderstandings.

It is not uncommon for students to arrive at school or to a class feeling like their challenges are overwhelming, they don't have enough energy to succeed, all they hear are criticisms, and they make too many mistakes. Everyone has days like that, but for students who continually face this and don't have the necessary coping skills, it can feel overwhelming. Thus, formative assessment in relation to noncognitive skills is essential in helping lift students up. It shows them that a learning gap is not a chasm and that like falling off a ladder, you can pick yourself back up. As with any learning, it is a step-by-step process that starts with your current locus and identifies progressive steps toward success. Students who are having difficulty start by labeling their feelings, reframing the situation, and mastering self-calming techniques. As each step is practiced and monitored, it is also assessed and reflected upon in a continuous feedback loop.

WEAVING IT WITHIN LEARNING

In the classroom, the best way to assess dispositions such as resilience, self-regulation, perseverance, and self-efficacy is to embed them directly into learning and assessing.

Mr. Andreesen starts with an entrance slip asking students to explain their incoming feelings and attitudes about today's topic or, alternatively, about the baggage they are bringing into class with them. Students can put this into a basket for the teacher's review, or if there is a higher level of trust in the classroom, these can be shared. Responses can range from Arnold's "I can't wait to learn about other livable planets I can move to" to Henrietta, who says her friends make her feel like she is from another planet. After a brief discussion to ascertain their attitudes toward learning, he asks students to imagine putting these feelings into a balloon or suitcase that they let go of. He returns to these at the end of class to discuss any lingering concerns and next steps. This simple intervention can smooth the path to teaching and learning or alternatively indicate a need for more intensive interventions.

In relation to regulating, modifying, and redirecting their frame of mind, students can be asked why their current one may not be working. What are the alternatives? What can they do to change it to something more acceptable or functional? Mr. Andreesen offers rating scales for the more common pressures. He takes the time to explain and discuss them. Then, students can indicate where they are at the start of class and monitor changes during class. For example

I hate school; I always fail.	I don't feel like I'm failing at this very moment.	I believe that if I seek help I can do better.
I'll never be able to learn all this.	Wow, I got four out of seven right on the miniquiz.	I can see evidence of learning mastery.

This can be customized to align with the learning outcomes and success criteria for today's lesson.

This topic means nothing to me.	I am beginning to see why this topic has value.	Yikes, this really does affect my life.
I know nothing about this topic.	I can tell you a few things about his idea.	I can make connections to things I already know.

ENSURING ACHIEVABLE GOALS

In most curriculum or units of instruction there are overarching or big-picture learning outcomes, such as

- Determine central ideas of a text, analyze how they are conveyed through details, and summarize the key concepts and ideas.

These need to be deconstructed into achievable learning outcomes with steps that are manageable by all students. For example, after the teacher demonstrates, provides strategies, and gives examples

1. Based on their knowledge, she decides the whole class will read the same text. Students post on lino their individual thoughts on the main idea of the reading.

2. In pairs or individually, students use a graphic organizer to show how the details in the reading support (or refute) the main ideas that have been posted. Questions and uncertainties are discussed.

3. Individually, students summarize the main ideas as supported by details, then partner or form a small like-minded group that presents their ideas to the class.

During their learning, students monitor their progress by annotating a learning tracker, as shown in Table 5.4.

TABLE 5.4   Annotated Learning Tracker

The Standard:
Learning Outcomes:
This is what I already know and can do about the standard or learning outcomes:
What questions or concerns do I have now about it?

What are my personal learning goals? What strategies can I use to achieve them?

My description of the main idea is:

This is my class's consensus on the main idea:

My graphic organizer looks like this:

I would summarize my learning this way:

What evidence have I demonstrated of my growth, learning, and mastery?

How can I use this learning in other classes and places?

By annotating the learning tracker, several restorative strategies are incorporated: Mastery and growth are emphasized, self-regulation is supported, topics can be made relevant to students, and students develop self-monitoring skills.

REASONABLE CHALLENGE

Exit slips can be effective in gaining insights into student learning as they summarize their outcomes. The questions below align with a variety of noncognitive skills and dispositions:

Brainpower: How did your thinking change about ____?

What do you know now that you didn't know before?

Application: How can someone use this new knowledge and skills?

Planning Skills: I want to learn more about_____ because_____

Here are the steps I can take:

Creativity: What questions would a superhero have about this?

Goal Tracker: How did you demonstrate achievement of the big-picture goal, the tapered goals?

Relevance and meaning have been identified as activators of learning and engagement. If the mission of schools is to maximize success for students, it is essential to recognize that all students learn, but each in their own way. Cyrus might have his nose buried in a book about gardening, while Samira is organizing a group to design and plant a school garden. Learning is engaging work when it has a clear purpose, relevant content, and real-world connections.

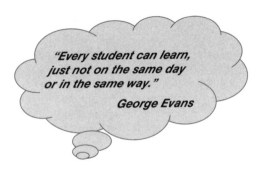

"Every student can learn, just not on the same day or in the same way."

George Evans

Reasonable challenge for some students means additional supports/scaffolds, alternative resources, extra time, or adaptation of assessments. One way to achieve this is through choice boards that are explained in Chapter 4. In this weighted example, students are expected to earn a specified number of points but can choose strategies that align with their abilities and interests. Table 5.5 shows ideas in multiple content areas. In this way, the level of appropriate challenge can be selected collaboratively by the student and teacher.

TABLE 5.5 Weighted Choice Board

POINTS	3	6	9
LEVEL OF LEARNING	REMEMBERING	APPLYING	CREATING
Choice 1	Prepare flash cards using Quizlet.	Write a story or song about a food's journey through your body.	Use a 3-D printer to produce left-handed scissors.
Choice 2	Draw pictures of the steps in photosynthesis for someone else to put into a sequence.	Use data to write an opinion piece on fracking.	Add new characters to the story and then write a different ending.
Choice 3	In a blog post, write directions for planting seeds.	Design a compare/ contrast chart or MindMup on seasons.	Develop a model of a technology of the future.

Reflection

Rather than waiting for big data to make big changes to teaching and learning, consider relying on small data to inform local adjustments to practice.

Think about/discuss with your team two ways you can merge the development of noncognitive skills with assessment in your classroom, grade level, or school.

What outcomes do you anticipate?

How will you respond to them?

INSIGHTS AND APPLICATION

Authorities in this area recommend that noncognitive skill building start in early childhood and be infused throughout the formative years, as its effects are long lasting. Farrington et al. (2014) found that it is not solely the skill building but that "promising adolescent interventions are those that target non-cognitive skills as well as offer mentoring, and guidance" (p. 8). Her University of Chicago study of noncognitive factors that shape school performance broadens the understanding of skills to also include attitudes, competencies, strategies, and behaviors. Out of numerous studies, conscientiousness, "the tendency to be organized, responsible, and hardworking, is the most predictive" of success (p. 23).

I learned about Sisu when I married into a family with Finnish heritage. It cannot be translated metaphrastically into English but encompasses the ideas of resilience, perseverance, grit, courage, and hardiness. People who exhibit it show equanimity in the face of stress, strive to overcome challenges, and demonstrate a mindset of taking action in tough situations. Overused, it can be translated into hardheadedness and inflexibility. As with any noncognitive trait, ability, or disposition, it should be balanced by reason and restraint.

Each of us sees the world through our own lens. Some prefer facts and data, others rely on their feelings, and some weigh potential obstacles and opportunities. Use the reflections in Table 5.6 to consider something you've read, viewed, or experienced in the classroom in relation to noncognitive skills and attributes.

TABLE 5.6 Perceptions and Reflections

THE LENS	YOUR REFLECTION
What happened? Explain using facts, data, information, actions, details, and so forth.	
What's wrong here? What errors were made? Why isn't it effective or won't it succeed?	
What's right here? What went well? What are the positive outcomes? Where can this lead?	
How do you feel? Describe your reactions, emotions, impressions, change of mood, and so on.	
What's next? What opportunities does this offer? How can I grow and improve as a result? What did I learn about myself or the issue/event/problem?	
Metacognition: Thinking about your thinking. Can you explain how you got to this point? Can you change your perspective? What can you do to take control or let it go?	

Summary and Significant Conclusions:

Lingering Questions:

CHAPTER 6

Conclusions and New Beginnings

Chapter Goals/Key Ideas
Return to the roots of assessment through principled and purposeful practice.
Cultivate a culture of assessment that is inclusive, comprehensive, and sustainable.
Unify policy with practice.
Upskill teachers' restorative practices and purposes.
Uplift students toward rising levels of mastery and success.
Partner with parents as informed advisers and consumers of assessment.

Restorative assessment relies on a spectrum of practice. There is not one effortless solution that fits and fixes every setting. Throughout this book, the ideas have intended to be descriptive rather than prescriptive.

Each school, district, and community must work together to establish local priorities, choose the best practices for their setting, prepare and support teachers with renewed perspectives on assessment, modify routines of practice, and engage all stakeholders in developing a plan to untangle the roots, nurture assessment, and sustain growth.

BECOMING UNSTUCK

Having explained the hard work of changing beliefs and practice, here is where you will find the steps to make it happen. Earlier in the book, we talk about assessment that is intentional, balanced, informative, equitable, growth oriented, and student centered, as well as assessment literacy and noncognitive skills for success. Let's explore how policy and practice further these ideas for underperforming, struggling, and stressed learners in restorative settings.

FACING CHALLENGES

I was in a meeting recently when a member of the group denied that income inequality has anything to do with academic achievement. He cited those who overcame obstacles and achieved success by hard work and self-reliance. I agree that these inspiring stories can be of value but also know that achievement is much more complicated. A convergence of convincing research and emerging data means that this is a great time to take steps in that direction. We know the effects of substandard living on academic success and the price that children pay when they are born into poverty. We also know that most parents dream of better outcomes for their children, yet many lack the knowledge, skills, and resources to achieve this goal. There is also evidence from the neurosciences and additional perspectives from the sociological and psychological literature, all of which can be used to inform thinking and propel change.

Students drop out of school mentally and emotionally before they leave physically. A report from the Center for Public Education (2005) describes factors that correlate with impending failure and dropping out. You can learn more about these ideas at the National Dropout Prevention Center/Network at Clemson University (n.d.). While dropout rates have been going down, we are far from being successful in helping every student succeed.

Holding teachers accountable for the dropout rate is like holding the chef accountable for someone's obesity. He can make the most delicious food, present it in a visually appealing way, engage the diners in conversation about their preferences, but cannot keep them from overeating.

Accountability doesn't mean rating teachers based on students' test scores. Accountability means being able to account for one's actions. It means adjusting the sails before the storm. In the classroom, it means dependable and authentic instruction, fair and balanced assessment, and the scaffolds and resources necessary for achievement.

The teachers I know already feel accountable to their students. Through their actions they show respect and fairness, offer relevant and engaging opportunities to learn, principled assessments of learning, and the structures to support all learners.

CONDITIONS FOR HIGH PERFORMANCE

Rather than seeking external quick fixes, we need to first look locally for solutions. In one setting, reducing absenteeism meant engaging and supporting parents. In another setting, it meant working with students to overcome barriers to attending school.

High-performing schools have several characteristics in common. Whether they are low or high resourced, they share these core beliefs and actions (based on the work of the Center for Public Education [2005]; Kannapel & Clements [2005], and West [2016]).

1. A culture of high expectations for everyone who is part of the school community.

2. Goals that focus on the development of each student rather than high-stakes test scores.

3. Emphasis on improvement, growth, and progress.

4. Spotlight on shared and strategic goals and focused learning outcomes.

5. Unity of purpose: This may be academic, noncognitive, or skill-based.

6. Development of students' higher-order thinking skills.

7. A safe, respectful, and caring community.

8. Student self-management, social awareness, and personal responsibility.

9. School leadership that is highly involved and dedicated to student success.

10. Communication, collaboration, and teamwork among teachers.

11. Informed and insightful responses to ongoing embedded assessments.

12. Use of "data" (used broadly) to improve instruction and adjust learning.

ROOTS AND WINGS

Somewhere between the two following statements lies the hinge point for building success locally:

1. We are so discriminated against. Without equal opportunity, our children don't have a chance to succeed in school.

2. If I can pull myself up by my bootstraps, then so can everyone else.

Despite or because of the urban schools I attended, I was given adequate opportunities to learn a lot of content knowledge. Although my father left school after the eighth grade, his mantra was persistent, loud, and clear: "My children will go to college." I did well on standardized tests, but it wasn't until college that I realized there was learning beyond memorizing facts. In turn, I became captivated by the process of analyzing, adapting, synthesizing, and creating, and more recently have extolled the importance of noncognitive foundations of learning.

Pisabay

We spend a lot of time following the latest fads and trends, whether they be STEAM, the three C's of twenty-first-century skills, or Common Core. There is a history of taking good ideas to the extreme, such as expecting teachers to differentiate lessons for every learner, or letting students decide how and what to learn, or making Homer's *Odyssey* required reading for all ninth graders.

We become unstuck when we rely on the research that informs best practice in assessment. It is how we return to the roots, purposes, and processes of good assessment. And when we do this, we can give wings to all learners: those who are reluctant, disengaged, gone astray, bored, and despondent.

NURTURE LOCAL CULTURE

Despite all the large-scale pressure to change, it is at the local level that transformation really happens. These are the pathways that require cultivation.

Values and Priorities: Systems that place a value on assessment, not just measurement, build a culture that sees assessments, both formative and summative, as opportunities for learning. We no longer live in a world where all content can be taught to all students. The complexity of science, the breadth of reading materials, and the magnitude of digital information changes the emphasis from content mastery to process mastery. Knowing what students know is less important than knowing how they analyze and utilize what they know.

Climate: Without a set plan to address an entire school climate and a process for dealing with problem behavior, school leaders may find themselves jumping to suspension or expulsion to deal with challenging students. Research shows that students subjected to exclusion are less likely to be engaged in the classroom and more likely to drop out of school. (Samuels, 2016, p. 2)

Strategies for strengthening school climate include co-construction of goals, shared emphasis on growth, positive behavior supports, respect, and safety (physical, social, and emotional).

System: These are systems of high expectations where failure is not an option. In these settings, scaffolds, support, and resources are available for learners who may need additional assistance to be successful. A culture of assessment means that multiple pathways to success and varied types of assessment are valued. A balanced approach to assessment is the norm.

Classrooms: Establish routines of learning where students feel safe taking risks—where it is okay to take informed guesses and try multiple strategies to solve a problem. In these classrooms, students are involved in tracking their learning. They are familiar with the goals and learning intentions, and can assess their own progress through the use of rubrics, contracts, and learning logs.

Teachers: Collegial and collaborative teaching is built on trust. Having an opportunity to turn to a colleague for ideas and encouragement promotes cooperation and minimizes isolation. When teachers are empowered and respected, they are motivated to continually improve their practice. These teachers are willing to try various paths to student success. Teachers don't get to select their raw materials as the manufacturing world does, nor is teaching an exact science as are pill formulation or engineering space launches. It is an opportunity to nurture each and every learner and build the skills necessary for his or her personal success.

UNIFY POLICY AND PRACTICE

When assessment is mastery based rather than time-bound, it doesn't mean there are endless opportunities to retest but rather that a balanced and comprehensive approach to assessment can benefit all learners. When multiple methods including a spectrum of strategies, from in-the-moment classroom assessment to large-scale national and international measures, are routinely used, then all students have opportunities to show improvement and demonstrate success. A comprehensive system means that assessment is informative in multiple ways: immediately in the classroom, locally at the school and district level, as well as for state and national policy makers.

TRANSLATING POLICY INTO PRACTICE

Start with the big picture: Fed by corporate interests, marginally-informed public officials, and pressure from personal interest groups, large-scale policy and standardized testing have taken control of education. But think about reversing this direction to "practice guides policy."

Flip the formula: Use what is known about best practice to inform policy. Rely on the best ideas from professionals and specialists in teaching, learning, and assessing, many of whom can be found in the reference section of this book as well as throughout your school.

Rely on the research: The key ideas of assessment—engaging, informative, reciprocal, and relevant to student and learning purposes—have gotten lost in heated conversations about which tests to use. Remember, a test is merely a strategy among a myriad of effective practices.

Be consistent: In restorative assessment, consistency is key. Rather than depending on ever-shifting standards, rely on visible and purposeful learning intentions. Incorporate these into effective and meaningful classroom routines, consistent behavioral expectations, and predictable responses. Revise and align behavioral supports with curriculum requirements and teacher evaluations.

Take it local: It is much easier to incorporate fairness and equity at the local level, where there is more flexibility in teaching, learning, and assessing This is where you can be innovative in ensuring that all learners have opportunities for improvement and success. Which is more important in understanding *Julius Caesar:* explaining "Et tu, Brute" as a literary device, answering a multiple-choice question on Flavius's job or comparing the plot to recent history.

COMMITTING TO BEST PRACTICE

Upskilling Teachers

Everyone likes to hear that they are good at what they do: From a child's first try at basketball to the winner of the National Spelling Bee, each of us is good at something. When Mr. O'Byrne asks his students, "What's your special power," he doesn't expect them to be supermen and superwomen but rather to think deeply about what they know and do. Marcus says that he can run so fast that his mother always picks him to go to the groceria for milk. Zyrla says he can do math in his head, and Odessa says she helps her friends when they have a problem.

Teachers also have special powers. Mr. O'Neal says he can listen to two students reading different texts at the same time, and Mrs. Davis convinces her students that with just "a little more oomph" they can succeed. I have never heard a teacher say their secret power is assessing. Why? Because typically, assessment means testing. Some even claim that testing, assessment, and evaluation can be used interchangeably.

Upskilling means teachers recognize the importance of gathering information (not just data) from multiple sources. It means delving into student displays of learning in order to develop a deep understanding of what they know, understand, and can do with their learning. This results in the use of assessment by teachers and students to improve learning.

Upskilled teachers ensure that the learning targets are clear to students, assessments are purposeful and aligned, and multiple measures gauge the outcomes of learning and guide next steps. Remember that when assessment is about the learner rather than the teacher, it becomes more relevant, engaging, and responsive.

Uplifting Learners

Beyond mastering content knowledge, students need to become independent learners who are willing and able to take on rigorous challenges requiring higher-level thinking. Students who have the greatest academic risks are the ones who have most to gain from restorative assessment. These are the learners who need to be uplifted from apathy and acceptance of failure to an attitude of progress and achievement. Keep in mind these are not only the socioeconomically disadvantaged but also include students who are overindulged, self-centered, elitist, demanding, and disrespectful.

Students may bring inaccurate information to their learning, which in turn impacts new learning. For example, students may come to class believing they are not good at writing or think that dinosaurs and humans lived on earth at the same time. It is important to assess incoming knowledge, skills, and readiness for learning, and to recognize how this can impact new learning. This in turn guides the ongoing strategies that are most relevant for introducing, mastering, and assessing new learning.

Students must know what they are expected to learn and how they will show their learning. If there are no street signs or trail markers, it is easy to get lost. Learners are more successful when they are provided with practical strategies to achieve mastery as well as ongoing monitoring of learning. Under these circumstances, students are more likely to reach their destination.

Nourish task-based motivation, responsible autonomy, and personal control. These multifaceted skills and dispositions have a powerful effect on educational outcomes. Success encourages further learning: Failure discourages it. Deconstruct learning goals and provide targeted feedback in order to nurture and acknowledge growth. In this way, students can see how their learning is improving on a day-by-day basis. Enrique did not believe he would finish his project on types of energy, but when Mr. Choi helped to deconstruct it into daily outcomes, he realized that small steps lead to bigger goals.

Boosting Leadership

The first important thing to understand about uplifting leadership is that it demands consistency between *what* you lead, *why* you lead, and *how* you lead. In uplifting leadership, the ends and means are inseparable. (Hargreaves & Boyle, 2015)

This journey takes hard work, persistence, and the support of others. It starts with shared understandings of assessment and a clear sense of the present and the future. It requires collaborative forward movement. Boosting leadership is not just providing a to-do list but rather offering airstreams that help them flow.

PARTNERING WITH PARENTS

Pisabay

Parents are a child's first teacher and the greatest influence on their children's school achievement. Dufur, Parcel, and Troutman (2013) found that strong "family social capital," meaning the bonds between parents and children such as trust, communication, and connectedness, correlated more highly with students' success than "school social capital," meaning climate, extracurricular, and personalization. At the same time, research shows that teachers are the most important school-based factor in student learning. Collectively, there is no doubt that both parents and teachers want what is best for every learner.

There are three key ideas when it comes to partnering with parents:

1. Working together is important for multiple reasons.

2. There are many pathways to building strong partnerships.

3. Schools have changed: Teaching, learning, and parenting are more complex.

ENGAGING PARENTS IN EDUCATION

Parents from diverse backgrounds can face the greatest barriers in connecting with the cultures and customs of schools. This is due to lack of transportation, working long hours to provide adequate housing, and understanding the norms and complexities of today's schools and classrooms.

Parents are more likely to get involved when they are encouraged through a sense of belonging or a personal invitation. Offer opportunities for them to participate and make a contribution, whether it be accompanying the class on a field trip, attending PTA meetings, or joining a committee to plan multicultural events.

IN PARTNERSHIP

Schools Can engage parents through these feasible steps and strategies:

1. Seek input from parents on how to best meet their child's needs and expectations.
2. Use multiple channels to communicate and share information about assessments.
3. Reach out to families through routine classroom and school updates.
4. Offer information on how parents can support the school's learning goals.
5. Send home information, in multiple languages, on effective parenting routines.
6. Make translators and translations available to improve communication.
7. Learn about cultural norms of the families in your school.
8. Provide opportunities for engagement at all levels of the system.
9. Provide regular updates on classroom, school, and district student-assessment activities.
10. Explain strategies for monitoring learning, testing, reporting, and responding.
11. Help parents understand the meaning of test scores.
12. Provide parent-friendly report cards.

Teachers Can: In addition to the schoolwide ideas and using the school's translators:

1. Contact parents about the positive accomplishments of their children.
2. Reach out to them early with concerns.
3. Acknowledge how homework improved with family involvement.
4. Send brief recaps of daily learning activities and their assessments.
5. Place brief notes, for both the parents and the student, on student work that is sent home.
6. Offer examples of ways that parents can extend their child's learning at home.

Engaging Parents: Ask them, either by survey or an information meeting, about the best ways to engage them in their child's learning. Ask about

1. aspirations for their child's academic achievement and routes to success;
2. their priorities for core learning (ELA, math, science) versus citizenship, creativity, digital literacy;
3. development of character traits, morality, self-discipline, self-esteem;
4. the value they place on the arts;
5. the importance of learning about diversity and multiculturalism;
6. questions regarding coping with peer pressure, setting limits, and other social skills;
7. beliefs about project-based learning;
8. concerns about standardized testing; and
9. suggestions for finding time for parents and teachers to work together.

A WIN-WIN FOR ALL

1. Parent involvement at home has a measurable impact on student performance and behavior.

2. Parent involvement reduces antisocial behaviors, violence, abuse, and bullying.

3. Early contact with parents is more likely to reduce absenteeism and increase academic achievement.

4. Opportunities are provided to shape important decisions about students.

5. By replacing the stress of testing with an understanding that assessment is about improvement, parents become robust partners.

6. From a big-picture perspective, engaging parents can improve school climate, behaviors, and outcomes.

APPLIED LEARNING

Work collaboratively to decide which elements of restorative assessment are most important to your students and community. Be sure your ideas are

- specific and relevant to the problem or goal;

- measurable and achievable in the available timeframe;

- clear and understandable to everyone involved;

- and incorporate success markers throughout the process, the necessary skills and resources that are available, and that there is continuous monitoring of progress and outcomes.

RESTORATIVE ASSESSMENT is the foundation of a purposeful and comprehensive assessment system. It is founded on a belief in the potential of all learners and anchored on research that supports best practice. Restoring assessment to its roots means being inclusive of all students, continuously monitoring and responding to learning, engaging assessment-capable learners, valuing the importance of noncognitive attributes, and ensuring equity for all students. Elaborate on what the ideas in this book mean to you.

RESTORING ASSESSMENT	STUDENT LEARNING INDICATORS	TEACHING ROUTINES	ASSESSMENT PRACTICES
REVERTING TO PURPOSE			
RESTORING BALANCE			
REINSTATING MASTERY AND GROWTH			
REFOCUSING ON LEARNERS			
RECONSIDERING NONCOGNITIVE SKILLS AND DISPOSITIONS			

References

Links to references are included to help you explore the topics in this book more deeply. Links to references are subject to change. Apologies for those that are no longer active.

Æsop. (2016). *The fox and the grapes*. In Æsop's Fables (p. 61). Hollywood, FL: Simon & Brown.

Ainsworth, L. (2010). *Rigorous curriculum design*. Englewood, CO: Lead & Learn Press.

Andrade, H., Huff, K., & Brooke, G. (2012). *Assessing learning*. Retrieved from http://studentsatthecenterhub.org/wp-content/uploads/2015/10/Assessing-Learning-Students-at-the-Center-1.pdf

Ausubel, D. (1968). *Educational psychology: A cognitive view*. New York, NY: Holt, Rinehart, & Winston.

Banta, T. W., & Palomba, C. A. (1999). *Assessment essentials: Planning, implementing, and improving assessment*. New York, NY, Jossey-Bass.

Black, P., & Wiliam, D. (1998a). *Assessment for learning: Beyond the black box*. Cambridge, England: University of Cambridge School of Education.

Black, P., & Wiliam, D. (1998b). Inside the black box: Raising standards through classroom assessment. *Phi Delta Kappan, 92*(1), 81-90.

Blackwell, L. S., Trzesniewski, K. H., & Dweck, C. S. (2007, January/February). Implicit theories of intelligence predict achievement across an adolescent transition: A longitudinal study and an intervention. *Child Development, 78*(1), 246–263. Retrieved from http://mtoliveboe.org/cmsAdmin/uploads/blackwell-theories-of-intelligence-child-dev-2007.pdf

Blankenship, A., Noguera, P., & Kelly, L. (2016). *Excellence through equity: Five principles of courageous leadership to guide achievement for every student*. Thousand Oaks, CA: Corwin.

Bloom, B. S. (1971). Mastery learning. In J. H. Block (Ed.), *Mastery learning: Theory and practice* (pp. 47–63). New York, NY: Holt, Rinehart & Winston.

Brewster, C., & Railsback, J. (2003). *Building trusting relationships for school improvement*. Retrieved from http://educationnorthwest.org/sites/default/files/trust.pdf

Briggs, D. C., Diaz-Bilello, E., Peck, F., Alzen, J., Chattergoon, R., & Johnson, R. (2015). *Using a learning progression framework to assess and evaluate growth*. Retrieved from http://www.colorado.edu/education/sites/default/files/attached-files/CADRE.CFA-StudentGrowthReport-Final_0.pdf

Brookhart, S. M., Andolina, M., Zuza, M., & Furman, R. (2004). Minute math: An action research study of student self-assessment. *Educational Studies in Mathematics, 57*, 213–227.

Bundick, M. J., Quaglia, R. J., Corso, M. J., & Haywood, D. (2014). Promoting student engagement in the classroom. *Teachers College Record, 116*(4). Retrieved from http://www.tcrecord.org/content.asp?contentid=17402

Butler, R. (1988). Enhancing and undermining intrinsic motivation: The effects of task-involved and ego-involved evaluation on interest and performance. *British Journal of Educational Psychology, 58*(1), 1–14.

Center for Public Education. (2005). *High-performing, high-poverty schools: Research review.* Retrieved from http://www.centerforpubliceducation.org/Main-Menu/Organizing-a-school/High-performing-high-poverty-schools-At-a-glance-/High-performing-high-poverty-schools-Research-review.html

Chabat, A., Rouxel, C., & Billot, A. (Producers), & Balmès, T. (Director). (2010). *Babies* [Documentary]. United States: Focus Features.

Chomsky, N. (2015). *Noam Chomsky on the dangers of high standardized testing* [Partial transcript of interview]. Retrieved from https://creativesystemsthinking.wordpress.com/2015/02/21/noam-chomsky-on-the-dangers-of-standardized-testing/

Churchill, A. (2015). *Bless the tests: Three reasons for standardized testing.* Retrieved from https://edexcellence.net/articles/bless-the-tests-three-reasons-for-standardized-testing

Clarke, S. (2001). *Unlocking formative assessment.* London, England: Trans-Atlantic Publications.

Coladarci, T. (2002, June). Is it a house or a pile of bricks? Important features of a local assessment system. *Phi Delta Kappan, 83*(10), 772–774.

Collins, R. (2014). Skills for the 21st century: Teaching higher-order thinking. *Curriculum and Leadership Journal, 12*(14). Retrieved from http://www.curriculum.edu.au/leader/teaching_higher_order_thinking,37431.html?issueID=12910

Conley, D. T. (2014). *Getting ready for college, careers, and the common core.* San Francisco, CA: Jossey-Bass.

Corcoran, T., Mosher, F.A., & Rogat, A. (2009). *Learning progressions in science: An evidence-based approach to reform.* Retrieved from http://www.cpre.org/images/stories/cpre_pdfs/lp_science_rr63.pdf

Costa, A., & Kallick, B. (Eds.). (2008). *Learning and leading with habits of mind: 16 essential characteristics for success.* Alexandria, VA: Association for Supervision & Curriculum Development.

Crooks, T. (1988). The impact of classroom evaluation practices on students. *Review of Educational Research, 58*(4), 438–481.

Csikszentmihalyi, M. (2008). *Flow: The psychology of optimal experience.* New York, NY: Harper Perennial Modern Classics.

Darling-Hammond, L. (2016). *Rise above the mark* [Video]. Jacklink Productions, Los Angeles, CA. Retrieved from https://riseabovethemark.com/

Darling-Hammond, L., Herman, J., Pellegrino, J., Abedi, J., Aber, J. L., Baker, E., . . . Steele, C.M. (2013). *Criteria for high-quality assessment.* Retrieved from https://edpolicy.stanford.edu/publications/pubs/847

Dietel, R. J., Herman, J. L., & Knuth, R. A. (1991). *What does research say about assessment?* Oak Brook, IL: North Central Regional Education Laboratory. Retrieved from http://www.education.umd.edu/EDMS/MARCES/mdarch/pdf/msde000013.pdf

Dufur, M. J., Parcel, T. L., & Troutman, K. P. (2013). Does capital at home matter more than capital at school? Social capital effects on academic achievement. *Research in Social Stratification and Mobility, 31,* 3.

Dweck, C. S. (2007). *Mindset: The new psychology of success*. New York, NY: Ballantine Books.

Dweck, C. S., & Leggett, E. L. (1988). A social-cognitive approach to motivation and personality. *Psychological Review, 95,* 256–273.

Dweck, C. S., Walton, M. W., & Cohen, G. L. (2014). *Academic tenacity: Mindsets and skills that promote long-term learning.* Retrieved from https://ed.stanford.edu/sites/default/files/manual/dweck-walton-cohen-2014.pdf

Duckworth, A. (2016). *Grit: The power of passion and perseverance*. New York, NY: Scribner.

Elementary and Secondary Education Act of 1965, as Amended by the Every Student Succeeds Act—Accountability and State Plans, 81 Fed. Reg. 34539 (May 31, 2016). Retrieved from https://www.federalregister.gov/articles/2016/05/31/2016-12451/elementary-and-secondary-education-act-of-1965-as-amended-by-the-every-student-succeeds

Farkas, G. (2003, August). Cognitive skills and non-cognitive traits and behaviors in stratification processes. *Annual Review of Sociology, 29,* 541–562.

Farrington, C. A. (2013). *Academic mindsets as a critical component of deeper learning.* Retrieved from http://www.howyouthlearn.org/pdf/White_Paper_Academic_Mindsets_as_a_Critical_Component_of_Deeper_Learning_Camille_Farrington_April_20_2013.pdf

Farrington, C. A., Roderick, M., Allensworth, E., Nagaoka, J., Keyes, T. S., Johnson, D. W., & Beechum, N. O. (2014). *Teaching adolescents to become learners. The role of noncognitive factors in shaping school performance: A critical literature review.* Chicago, IL: University of Chicago Consortium on Chicago School Research.

Fernandes, M., & Fontana, D. (1996). Changes in control beliefs in Portuguese primary school pupils as a consequence of the employment of self-assessment strategies. *British Journal of Educational Psychology, 66*(3), 301–313.

Fisher, D., & Frey, N. (2009). Feed up, back, forward. *Educational Leadership, 67*(3), 20–25.

Fried, R. (2001). *The passionate teacher: A practical guide*. Boston, MA: Beacon Press.

Frymier, J., & Gansneder, B. (1989). The Phi Delta Kappa study of students at risk. *Phi Delta Kappan, 71,* 142–146.

Glossary of Education Reform. (n.d.). At-risk. Retrieved from www.edglossary.org

Gong, B. (2010). *Using balanced assessment systems to improve student learning and school capacity.* Retrieved from http://www.ccsso.org/Documents/Balanced Assessment Systems GONG.pdf

Greenstein, L. (2012). *Assessing 21st century skills: A guide to evaluating mastery and authentic learning*. Thousand Oaks, CA: Corwin.

Gutman, L. M., & Schoon, I. (2013). *The impact of non-cognitive skills on outcomes for young people*. London, England: Institute of Education, University of London.

Gyllander, L. (2012). *Developing a reciprocal assessment practice through teacher and student collaboration.* Retrieved from http://www.aare.edu.au/publications-database.php/6599/developing-a-reciprocal-assessment-practice-through-teacher-and-student-collaboration

Hargreaves, A., & Boyle, A. (2015). Improving schools: What works? *Educational Leadership, 72*(5), 42–47.

Hattie, J. (n.d.). *Visible learning*. Retrieved from https://visible-learning.org/

Hattie, J. (2009). *Visible learning: A synthesis of over 800 meta-analyses relating to achievement.* New York, NY: Routledge.

Hattie, J. (2011). *Visible learning for teachers*. New York, NY: Routledge.

Hattie, J., & Donoghue, G. M. (2016). Learning strategies: A synthesis and conceptual model. *NPJ Science of Learning, 1*. doi:10.1038/npjscilearn.2016.13

Headden, S., & McKay, S. (2015). *Motivation matters: How new research can help teachers boost student engagement.* Stanford, CA: Carnegie Foundation for the Advancement of Teaching. Retrieved from https://www.carnegiefoundation.org/resources/publications/motivation-matters-how-new-research-can-help-teachers-boost-student-engagement/

Heckman, J. J., & Kautz, T. D. (2012). *Hard evidence on soft skills.* Retrieved from http://www.nber.org/papers/w18121.pdf

Heritage, M. (2008). *Learning progressions: Supporting instruction and formative assessment.* Los Angeles: National Center for Research on Evaluation, Standards, and Student Testing, and University of California. Retrieved from http://www.k12.wa.us/assessment/ClassroomAssessmentIntegration/pubdocs/FASTLearningProgressions.pdf

Hess, K. (2008). *Developing and using learning progressions as a schema for measuring progress.* Retrieved from http://www.nciea.org/publications/CCSSO2_KH08.pdf

Huba, M. E., & Freed, J. E. (2000). *Learner-centered assessment on college campuses: Shifting the focus from teaching to learning.* Boston, MA: Allyn & Bacon.

Immordino-Yang, M. H. (2015). *Emotions, learning, and the brain: Exploring the educational implications of affective neuroscience.* New York, NY: Norton.

Joint Committee on Standards for Educational Evaluation. (2015). *The Classroom Assessment Standards for PreK–12 Teachers.* Retrieved from http://www.jcsee.org/the-classroom-assessment-standards-new-standards

Jones, D. E., Greenberg, M., & Crowley, M. (2015). Early social-emotional functioning and public health: The relationship between kindergarten social competence and future wellness. *American Journal of Public Health, 105*(11), 2283–2290. Retrieved from https://www.ncbi.nlm.nih.gov/pmc/articles/PMC4605168/

Kannapel, P. J., & Clements, S. K. (2005). *Inside the black box of high-performing high-poverty schools.* Retrieved from http://people.uncw.edu/kozloffm/highperforminghighpoverty.pdf

Kautz, T., Heckman, J. J., Diris, R., Weel, B., & Borghans, L. (2014). *Fostering and measuring skills: Improving cognitive and non-cognitive skills to promote lifetime success.* Paris, France: Organisation for Economic Co-operation and Development. Retrieved from https://www.oecd.org/edu/ceri/Fostering-and-Measuring-Skills-Improving-Cognitive-and-Non-Cognitive-Skills-to-Promote-Lifetime-Success.pdf

Klein, A., (2016). *John King calls for emphasis on educational equity in new ESSA era.* Retrieved from http://blogs.edweek.org/edweek/campaign-k-12/2016/01/john_king_to_call_for_emphasis.html

Klenowski, V. (1995). Student self-evaluation processes in student-centered learning contexts of Australia and England. *Assessment in Education, 2*(2), 145–163.

Kyllonen, P. C. (2005, September). The case for noncognitive assessments. *R & D Connections,* 1–7.

Lea, S., Stephenson, D., & Troy, J. (2003). Higher education students' attitudes to student-centred learning: Beyond 'educational bulimia'? *Studies in Higher Education, 28*(3), 321–334.

Lemann, N. (1995). The great sorting. *Atlantic Monthly, 276*(3), 84–100.

Linquanti, R. (2014). *Supporting formative assessment for deeper learning: A primer for policymakers.* Washington, DC: Council of Chief State School Officers. Retrieved from http://www.ccsso.org/Documents/Supporting%20Formative%20Assessment%20for%20Deeper%20Learning.pdf

Mangels, J. A., Butterfield, B., Lamb, J., Good, C. D., & Dweck, C. S. (2006). Why do beliefs about intelligence influence learning success? A social cognitive neuroscience model. *Social Cognitive and Affective Neuroscience, 1,* 75–86.

Marzano, R. (2007). *The art and science of teaching.* Alexandria, VA: Association for Supervision and Curriculum Development.

Maslow, A. H. (1943). A theory of human motivation. *Psychological Review, 50*(4), 370–396. Retrieved from http://psychclassics.yorku.ca/Maslow/motivation.htm

Maslow, A. H. (1954). *Motivation and personality.* New York, NY: Harper.

Masters, D. (n.d.). *Know thy impact: 4 questions to help you pin down what children are really learning.* Retrieved from http://visiblelearningplus.com/content/know-thy-impact-4-questions-help-you-pin-down-what-children-are-really-learning

McDonald, T. P., Calderone, S. M., Bergman, N., & Boyd, J. L. (2015). *Supporting statewide academic success through best practices.* Retrieved from http://www.wsac.wa.gov/sites/default/files/2016 College Readiness Brief Contracted Final (002).pdf

McMillan, J. (2012). *SAGE handbook of research on classroom assessment.* Thousand Oaks, CA: Sage.

National Center for Educational Statistics. (2015). *Knowledge and skills of first-time kindergarteners.* Retrieved from https://nces.ed.gov/fastfacts/display.asp?id=680

National Council on Measurement in Education. (1995). Code of professional responsibility in education. Retrieved from https://www.ncme.org/ncme/NCME/NCME/Resource_Center/LibraryItem/Code_of_Professional_Responsibilitie.aspx

National Dropout Prevention Center/Network at Clemson University. (n.d.). *Situations that put youth at risk.* Retrieved from http://dropoutprevention.org/resources/statistics/situations-that-put-youth-at-risk/

National Research Council. (2001). *Knowing what students know: The science and design of educational assessment.* Washington, DC: National Academies Press.

National Scientific Council on the Developing Child. (2015). *Excessive stress disrupts the architecture of the developing brain.* Cambridge, MA: Center on the Developing Child, Harvard University. Retrieved from http://46y5eh11fhgw3ve3ytpwxt9r.wpengine.netdna-cdn.com/wp-content/uploads/2005/05/Stress_Disrupts_Architecture_Developing_Brain-1.pdf

Northwest Evaluation Association. (2012). *For every child, multiple measures. What parents and educators want from K–12 assessments.* Retrieved from https://www.nwea.org/content/uploads/2014/07/NWEA-GRUNWALD_Assessment_Perceptions_b.pdf

Northwest Evaluation Association. (2016). *Make assessment work for all students: Multiple measures matter.* Retrieved from https://www.nwea.org/content/uploads/2016/05/Make_Assessment_Work_for_All_Students_2016.pdf

Obama administration announces new testing limits [Video file]. (2015). Retrieved from http://www.cnn.com/videos/us/2015/10/24/president-obama-school-testing-limits-students-arne-duncan-bpr-nr.cnn

Organisation for Economic Co-operation and Development. (2005). *Formative assessment: Improving learning in secondary classrooms.* Retrieved from http://www.oecd.org/edu/ceri/35661078.pdf

Ormrod, J. E. (2006). *Educational psychology: Developing learners* (6th ed.). Englewood Cliffs, NJ: Prentice Hall.

Pane, J. F., Steiner, E. D., Baird, M. D., & Hamilton, L. S. (2015). *Continued progress: Promising evidence on personalized learning.* Retrieved from http://k12education.gatesfoundation.org/wp-content/uploads/2015/11/Gates-ContinuedProgress-Nov13.pdf

Patall, E. A., Cooper, H., & Robinson, J. (2008). The effect of choice on intrinsic motivation and related outcomes: A meta-analysis of research findings. *Psychological Bulletin, 134*(2), 280–300.

Popham, J. (1999). *Why standardized tests don't measure educational quality.* Retrieved from http://www.ascd.org/publications/educational-leadership/mar99/vol56/num06/Why-Standardized-Tests-Don't-Measure-Educational-Quality.aspx

RAND Corporation. (2012). *Teachers matter: Understanding teachers' impact on student achievement.* Retrieved from http://www.rand.org/pubs/corporate_pubs/CP693z1-2012-09.html

Rieg, S. (2007, December). Classroom assessment strategies: What do students at-risk and teachers perceive as effective and useful? *Journal of Instructional Psychology, 34*(4), 214–225. Retrieved from http://www.freepatentsonline.com/article/Journal-Instructional-Psychology/173375578.html

Rimm-Kaufman, S., & Sandilos, L. (2011). *Improving students' relationships with teachers to provide essential supports for learning.* Retrieved from http://www.apa.org/education/k12/relationships.aspx

Rosen, J. A., Glennie, E. J., Dalton, B. W., Lennon, J. M., & Boznik, R. N. (2010). *Noncognitive skills in the classroom: New perspectives on educational research.* Research Triangle Park, NC: RTI International. Retrieved from https://www.rti.org/sites/default/files/resources/bk-0004-1009-rosen.pdf

Ross, J. A. (2006, November). The reliability, validity, and utility of self-assessment. *Practical Assessment Research and Evaluation, 11*(10), 1–13.

Sadler, D. R. (1989). Formative assessment and the design of instructional systems. *Instructional Science, 18*(2), 119–144.

Samuels, C. A. (2016, September 27). Tackling school climate, student behavior has a route to improvement. Retrieved from http://www.edweek.org/ew/articles/2016/09/28/tackling-school-climate-student-behavior-as-a.html?cmp=eml-enl-tu-news2

Scriven, M. (1967). The methodology of evaluation. In R. W. Tyler, R. M. Gagne, & M. Scriven (Eds.), *Perspectives of curriculum evaluation* (pp. 39–83). Chicago, IL: Rand McNally.

Shepard, L. A. (2000). *The role of classroom assessment in teaching and learning* (CSE Technical Report 517). Boulder: Center for Research on Evaluation, Standards, and Student Testing, and University of Colorado at Boulder. Retrieved from http://cresst.org/wp-content/uploads/TECH517.pdf

Simone, J. (2012). *Addressing the marginalized student: The secondary principal's role in eliminating deficit thinking* [Doctoral dissertation]. University of Illinois at Urbana-Champaign, Urbana, IL. Retrieved from https://www.ideals.illinois.edu/bitstream/handle/2142/31100/Simone_Joseph.pdf?sequence=1

Stobart, G. (2005). Fairness in multicultural assessment systems. *Assessment in Education, 12*(3), 275–287.

Strauss, V. (2016, May 9). "Big Data" was supposed to fix education. It didn't. It's time for "small data" [Web log post by P. Sahlberg & J. Hasak]. Retrieved from https://www.washingtonpost.com/news/answer-sheet/wp/2016/05/09/big-data-was-supposed-to-fix-education-it-didnt-its-time-for-small-data/

Suskie, L. (2000, May). *Fair assessment practices: Giving students equitable opportunities to demonstrate learning.* Retrieved from http://uncw.edu/cas/documents/FairAssessmentPractices_Suskie.pdf

Tomlinson, C. A., & Moon, T. R. (2013). Differentiation and classroom assessment. In J. H. McMillan (Ed.), *SAGE handbook of research on classroom assessment* (pp. 415–430). Thousand Oaks, CA: Sage.

Tschannen-Moran, M. (2014). *Trust matters: Leadership for successful schools* (2nd ed.). New York, NY: Wiley.

United Nations Educational, Scientific and Cultural Organization. (1950). *Statement by experts on race problems.* Retrieved from http://unesdoc.unesco.org/images/0012/001269/126969eb.pdf

Vohs, K., & Baumeister, R. F. (2012, July). Motivation, personal beliefs, and limited resources all contribute to self-control. *Journal of Experimental Social Psychology, 48*(4), 943–947.

Von Stumm, S., Hell, B., & Chamorro-Premuzic. (2011, November). The hungry mind: Intellectual curiosity is the third pillar of academic performance. *Perspectives on Psychological Science, 6*(6). Retrieved from http://pps.sagepub.com/content/6/6/574

Webb, N. (2002, April 1–5) *Assessment literacy in a standards-based urban education setting.* Paper presented at the American Educational Research Association Annual Meeting, New Orleans, LA. Retrieved from http://archive.wceruw.org/mps/AERA2002/Assessment%20literacy%20NLW%20Final%2032602.pdf

West, M. R. (2016). *Should non-cognitive skills be included in school accountability systems? evidence from California's CORE districts.* Washington, DC: Brookings Institution. Retrieved from https://www.brookings.edu/research/should-non-cognitive-skills-be-included-in-school-accountability-systems-preliminary-evidence-from-californias-core-districts/

Wiliam, D. (2011). *Embedded formative assessment.* Bloomington, IN: Solution Tree.

Index

Note: In page references, t indicates tables.

anagram, 28–29
assessment-capable learners and, 90–91
assessment viewed from multiple perspectives and, 52
at-risk students and, 11
balance and, 42
belief in, 45
changing assessment mindsets and, 87
clarity of purpose/outcomes and, 80
classroom guidelines for, 27
emotional well-being and, 28
equity and, 7
failure and, 40
fairness and, 35
flexibility/choice and, 110–111
foundation for, 43
growth measures and, 85
internal accountability and, 5
learning progressions and, 70
mastery learning and, 66, 67
mastery learning/formative assessment
    and, 82
motivation and, 47
multiple measures and, 50–51
multiple pathways to, 141
necessary supports for, 8
noncognitive skills and, 114, 116, 117, 126, 128,
    133, 135
opportunities/supports for, 25
pathways to, 10–11
real assessment and, 3
reasonable learning progressions and, 49
reflections on, 47
research-based practices and, 21
restorative assessment and, 4, 62
self-assessment and, 95
skills and, 114–116
social-emotional competencies that support, 36
trust/respect and, 23–24
Summative assessments, 41
Summit Schools, 11
Suskie, L., 34
Symbols, 34

Taxonomies, 55–56
    assessing levels of, 57t
    in practice, 59
Teachers:
    accountability and, 138–139
    assessment literacy and, 18
    collaborative teaching and, 141

fairness and, 34
importance of, 144
left behind, 4
most effective, 17
prepare/support, 137
real assessment and, 2–3
reciprocity between students and, 3
response by, 9
supportive, 5
trust/respect and, 23–24
upskilling, 142–143
white female, 5
Technology-based learning, 41
Testing:
    assessment and, 142
    mistaken idea of, 26
    parent involvement and, 146
    See also Assessment(s); High-stakes testing;
        Standardized testing
Title I, 127
Tomlinson, C. A., 107
Troutman, K. P., 144
Troy, J., 90
Truancy, 9
Trust:
    building, 6
    collaborative teaching and, 141
    continuous assessments and, 46
    mutual accountability and, 23–24
    noncognitive skills and, 118, 131
    parents and, 144
    in restorative classrooms, 27
    testing and, 26
Tschannen-Moran, M., 24

United Nations Educational, Scientific and Cultural
    Organization, 5

Validity:
    diverse views on, 31–32
    restorative, 32–33
    technically sound assessment and, 30–31
Violence:
    parent involvement and, 146
    stress and, 35
    success and, 40

Walton, M. W., 124
Webb, N., 17
Wiliam, D., 81

A SAGE Publishing Company

Helping educators make the greatest impact

CORWIN HAS ONE MISSION: to enhance education through intentional professional learning.

We build long-term relationships with our authors, educators, clients, and associations who partner with us to develop and continuously improve the best evidence-based practices that establish and support lifelong learning.

Solutions you want. Experts you trust. Results you need.

AUTHOR CONSULTING

Author Consulting

On-site professional learning with sustainable results! Let us help you design a professional learning plan to meet the unique needs of your school or district. www.corwin.com/pd

INSTITUTES

Institutes

Corwin Institutes provide collaborative learning experiences that equip your team with tools and action plans ready for immediate implementation. www.corwin.com/institutes

ECOURSES

eCourses

Practical, flexible online professional learning designed to let you go at your own pace. www.corwin.com/ecourses

READ2EARN

Read2Earn

Did you know you can earn graduate credit for reading this book? Find out how: www.corwin.com/read2earn